W. C. Fields —
An Annotated Guide

W. C. Fields — An Annotated Guide

Chronology, Bibliographies, Discography, Filmographies, Press Books, Cigarette Cards, Film Clips and Impersonators

David T. Rocks

McFarland & Company, Inc., Publishers
Jefferson, North Carolina

The present work is a reprint of the library bound edition of W.C. Fields — An Annotated Guide: Chronology, Bibliographies, Discography, Filmographies, Press Books, Cigarette Cards, Film Clips and Impersonators, *first published in 1993 by McFarland.*

LIBRARY OF CONGRESS CATALOGUING-IN-PUBLICATION DATA

Rocks, David T., 1937–
W. C. Fields — an annotated guide : chronology, bibliographies, discography, filmographies, press books, cigarette cards, film clips and impersonators / David T. Rocks.
p. cm.
Includes index.

ISBN 978-0-7864-7748-7
softcover : acid free paper ♾

1. Fields, W. C., 1879–1946. I. Title.
PN2287.F45R6 2014
016.79143'028'092 — dc20 92-56688

BRITISH LIBRARY CATALOGUING DATA ARE AVAILABLE

On the cover: W.C. Fields, circa 1938 (Photofest)

Manufactured in the United States of America

McFarland & Company, Inc., Publishers
Box 611, Jefferson, North Carolina 28640
www.mcfarlandpub.com

to my wife, Connie

ACKNOWLEDGMENTS

Grateful acknowledgment is made to: Margaret Herrick Library, Academy of Motion Picture Arts and Sciences; Periodicals section, Los Angeles Public Library; USC Cinema Collection, Doheny Memorial Library; Theater Arts Collection, UCLA University Research Library; Billy Rose Theatre Collection, N.Y.P.L. Lincoln Center; Memorial Library, University of Wisconsin, Madison; Motion Picture Section, The Library of Congress; Louis B. Mayer Library, American Film Institute; Hoblitzelle Theatre Arts Library, University of Texas; Theater Reference Department, Long Beach Public Library.

Thanks also go to John Behrens, CBS; Arthur Birsh, *Playbill;* Thomas J. Dady; Donald Deschner; Will Fowler; Beverly Hamer; Jud Hurd, *Cartoonist Profiles;* Rickey Jay; Ted Joyce; Judith Kass; Miles Krueger; John K. McLaughlin, The Book Sail; Michael Silverman, *Daily Variety;* Donald Stubblebine; Jan Tonnesen, Wahrenbrock's Book House; John Van Doren; J. Tim Walker; Jan Wall.

Photos are by Jim Hastings.

CONTENTS

INTRODUCTION

This is the most comprehensive bibliography of Fieldsiana yet compiled. Its unique features are the breadth of coverage and the thorough documentation of Fields' careers in the chronology. The chronology pinpoints every important aspect of Fields' four careers; juggler, vaudevillian, actor, and radio star. Although the main purpose of the bibliography is to provide the user with a reliable guide to the research materials that presently exist, critical annotations are given when necessary. To insure accuracy, full titles and subtitles have been recorded, and full pagination is given for every entry. Books containing Fields material have been annotated with page numbers locating the data pertaining to Fields. Books not indexed by their publishers also have been collated and indexed for the research guide. This feature allows the user to go directly to the Fields material. Periodicals containing Fields material also provide full pagination so that the user may see the exact length of an article, and thereby determine whether the article may or may not serve his or her purpose.

Press books are the richest source of information relating to movies. They provide data not easily obtainable elsewhere, such as advertising accessories used to promote a film.

The Fields cartoon filmography is completely unique to this book as is the section relating to cigarette cards.

Abbreviations have been used sparingly. Only two unusual words are used, olio and limning. An olio consists of the shorter parts of a long program. The olio usually includes the variety acts of song and dance, comic skits, juggling, and closing dramas. A limning is a drawing. Cartoonists refer to their drawings as limnings.

Overall, the user will find that this research guide is the most reliable source of data relating to the careers of W. C. Fields.

CHRONOLOGY

1. Jan. 29, 1880. Philadelphia, Pennsylvania. Fields was born Claude William Dukenfield.

2. May 13, 1898. Philadelphia. Fields performed in a fund-raising benefit for himself at Batley's Hall.[1]

3. May 14, 1898. Fields' first *New York Clipper* ad was published in the post office column, "Gentlemen's List," the day after his appearance at Batley's Hall.

4. Date? Norristown, Pennsylvania. Flynn & Grant's Park (also called Plymouth Park).

5. Date? Atlantic City, New Jersey. Fortesque's Pavillion.

*Although supporting documents have not been discovered it is generally conceded that Flynn & Grant's Park was Fields' first engagement after the Batley's Hall Performance. This was followed by his unusual engagement in Atlantic City (Taylor 42). When interviewed by Bernard Soble, Fields stated that he went to Atlantic City by way of Norristown, Pennsylvania (*Burleyque *116).*

6. Sept. 3, 1898. Report from the *New York Clipper* [stated] that the Monte Carlo Girls would open their season on September 19th and Manager James C. Fulton hired W. T. Bryant (late of Bryant and Richmond).

7. Sept. 10, 1898. J. C. Fulton wrote, as a result of his ad in the *New York Clipper*, Theo. H. Metz was hired as musical director of the Monte Carlo Girls.[2]

The following was Fields' weekly itinerary as published in the New York Clipper *from October 1, 1898, to February 2, 1901:*

8. Oct. 1, 1898. Gaiety Theatre (Albany, New York). Star Theatre (Troy, New York). "The olio included the Fulton Bros., Wm. C. Fields, Eva Swinburne, W. T. Bryant. . . .

9. Oct. 8, 1898. Unique Theatre (Brooklyn, New York). "William C. Fields. . . .

10. Oct. 15, 1898. Hersker's Opera House (Mahanoy City, Pennsylvania). "Monte Carlo Girls. . . ."

11. Oct. 22, 1898. Wonderland Theatre (Easton, Pennsylvania). Gaiety Theatre (Scranton, Pennsylvania). "Monte Carlo Girls. . . ."

12. Nov. 9, 1898. New Mountain Theatre (Altoona, Pennsylvania). "The Monte Carlo Girls [appeared the] week of 7th–12th. They had originally booked for only three days, but attendance was such as warranted their remaining the rest of the week."

Neither Fields nor the Monte Carlo Girls were mentioned in the New York Clipper *between November 14, 1898, and January 16, 1899. This was the winter in which the troupe disbanded and Fields was stranded in Kent, Ohio.*[3]

13. Jan. 28, 1899. Miner's Bowery Theatre (New York City). "The Monte Carlo Girls were seen here for the first time . . . opening January 22nd. W. C. Fields, tramp juggler, mingled comedy with dexterity."

14. Feb. 11, 1899. Gaiety Theatre (Troy, New York). Palace Theatre (Boston, Massachusetts). "In the olio were the Fulton Brothers, Wm. C. Fields in his wonderful juggling act, his first appearance in Boston."

15. Feb. 18, 1899. Unique Theatre (Brooklyn, New York). "Notes from the Monte Carlo Girls Burlesque Co. . . . booked solid until June 10th, playing week stands only."

16. Feb. 25, 1899. Becker's Lyceum Theatre (Reading, Pennsylvania). "In the olio . . . the Fulton Bros., W. C. Fields."

17. March 4, 1899. "The Monte Carlo Girls . . . now under the direction of Harlan and Garrick, with James F. Woods as manager. The Fulton Brothers are no longer with the company."

18. March 18, 1899. Rich's Theatre (Fall River, Massachusetts). "The Monte Carlo Girls [week of] 6–8." Music Hall (Lowell, Massachusetts). "The Monte Carlo Girls Company [week of] 9–11."

19. April 1, 1899. New Theatre (Lawrence, Massachusetts). Gaiety Theatre (Albany, New York). "W. G. [*sic*] Fields. . . ."

20. April 8, 1899. Olympic Theatre (Harlem, New York). "The olio includes Wm. C. Fields. . . ."

21. April 15, 1899. Gaiety Theatre (Scranton, Pennsylvania). "Monte Carlo Girls week of the 10th. . . ."

22. April 29, 1899. Unique Theatre (Brooklyn, New York). "And in the closing burlesque . . . Wm. C. Fields." Bijou Theatre (Binghamton, New York). "The Monte Carlo Girls [week of] 20–22."

23. May 1, 1899. London Theatre (New York City). "Wm. C. Fields, the tramp juggler in laughable tricks. . . ."

24. May 6, 1899. "Charles E. Taylor, for the past thirty weeks business manager of Fred Irwin's Majestic Burlesquers, is now general manager of the Monte Carlo Girls Burlesquers. He has added new acts to the olio and has written a new burlesque. Roster includes William C. Fields. . . ."

25. May 13, 1899. Waldmann's Opera House (Newark, New Jersey). "The Monte Carlo Girls."

26. May 20, 1899. Bijou Theatre (Paterson, New Jersey). "The Parisian Belles Gay Burlesquers will occupy stage [on the] 15th, instead of the Monte Carlo Girls as previously announced."

27. May 27, 1899. Kernan's Lyceum Theatre (Washington, D.C.). "Charles E. Taylor is now sole manager of the Monte Carlo Girls Burlesquers. The season will close June 10th at Monumental Theatre, Baltimore, Maryland."

28. June 3, 1899. Trocadero (Philadelphia, Pennsylvania). "The Monte Carlo Girls . . . on Saturday of last week Byron C. Harlan (and others of the troupe) issued an attachment against their manager, James C. Fulton, and garnished all the money due the company."

29. June 10, 1899. "Hines and Remington were hurriedly engaged late last Monday . . . at the Lyceum Theatre, Washington, D.C., filling out the week in place of the Monte Carlo Girls who did not appear."

30. July 8, 1899. "Notes from Murphy and Gibson's American Minstrels." "We opened at the Steel Pier, Atlantic City, N.J., June 26, for 12 weeks. John E. Murphy and Alf S. Gibson are proprietors and managers. The company includes . . . Wm. C. Fields. . . ."

31. July 29, 1899. "Wm. C. Fields, juggler, has closed 4 weeks engagement at the new Steel Pier, Atlantic City, N.J., and is now rehearsing with Irwin Brothers Burlesquers. He is engaged for the season."[4]

32. Aug. 26, 1899. People's Theater (Cincinnati, Ohio). "Irwin Bros., Burlesquers. . . ."

33. Sept. 9, 1899. Empire Theatre (Indianapolis, Indiana). "Irwin's Burlesquers [August] 28–Sept. 2."

34. Sept. 16, 1899. Star Theatre (Milwaukee, Wisconsin). "Irwin's Burlesquers opened this house . . . Sunday, [the] 10th."

35. Sept. 23, 1899. Trocadero (Chicago, Illinois). "Irwin's Burlesquers."

36. Oct. 7, 1899. Star Theatre (Cleveland, Ohio). "The olio, with which the show opened was good and included W. C. Fields, tramp juggler. . . ."

37. Oct. 28, 1899. Miner's Eighth Avenue Theatre (New York City). "Irwin's Burlesquers . . . appeared for the first time locally on Monday, Oct. 23rd. . . . Opened with an olio of specialties . . . W. C. Fields." Gaiety Theatre (Albany, New York). "The people receiving the most applause were . . . W. C. Fields. . . ." Star Theatre (Troy, New York). "Irwin's Burlesquers [week of] 19–21."

38. Nov. 4, 1899. Miner's Bowery Theatre (New York City). "Irwin's Burlesquers opened Oct. 30. The specialties were produced by . . . W. C. Fields."

39. Nov. 11, 1899. Empire Theatre (Brooklyn, New York). "Manager Clark presents Irwin's Burlesquers. [In] the olio . . . W. C. Fields, the tramp juggler."

40. Nov. 18, 1899. Star Theatre (Brooklyn, New York). "An olio which included W. C. Fields."

41. Nov. 25, 1899. Monumental Theatre (Baltimore, Maryland). "Irwin's Burlesquers did well [week of] 20–25."

42. Dec. 2, 1899. Lyceum Theatre (Washington, D.C.). "Irwin's Burlesquers."

43. Dec. 16, 1899. Trocadero (Philadelphia, Pennsylvania). "Olio included W.C. Fields."

44. Dec. 23, 1899. Miner's Eighth Avenue Theatre (New York City). "W. C. Fields."

45. Dec. 30, 1899. Miner's Bowery Theatre (New York City). "W. C. Fields juggled in tramp make up, introducing some laughable tricks."

46. Jan. 13, 1900. Gaiety Theatre (Albany, New York). "Irwin's Burlesquers . . . [week of Jan.] 1–3 . . . W. C. Fields." Star Theatre (Troy, New York). "Irwin Bros. Burlesquers drew well [Jan.] 4–6."

47. Jan. 27, 1900. People's Theatre (Cincinnati, Ohio). Grand Opera House (Marion, Ohio). "Irwin Bros. Specialty Co., came Jan. 13."

48. Feb. 3, 1900. Buckingham Theatre (Louisville, Kentucky). "Second time this season . . . in the olio . . . W. C. Fields."

49. Feb. 10, 1900. Empire Theatre (Indianapolis, Indiana). "Irwin's Burlesquers last week. . . ."

50. Feb. 17, 1900. Standard Theatre (St. Louis, Missouri). "Irwin's Burlesquers earned good money at manager Buttar's playhouse. This week [they] are here."

51. Feb. 24, 1900. Miaco's Trocadero (Chicago, Illinois). "Among the performers were W. C. Fields, tramp juggler. . . ."

52. March 3, 1900. "W. C. Fields will leave Fred Irwin's Burlesquers March 12, in Buffalo, N.Y., closing his thirtieth week. He will open on Orpheum circuit, March 18, in San Francisco, Cal."

53. March 24, 1900. "Latest by telegraph—Monday Night's Openings in all the Big Show Towns—Golden Gate Gleanings. Orpheum: The current bill . . . W. C. Fields."

54. April 14, 1900. Orpheum Theatre (San Francisco, California). "W. C. Fields was held over for a third week at the Orpheum Theatre. . . . He will play Los Angeles, Kansas City, and close on the circuit at Omaha May 12."

55. April 21, 1900. Orpheum Theatre (Los Angeles, California). "[Week of Jan.] 9. W. C. Fields."

56. May 12, 1900. Orpheum Theatre (Kansas City, Missouri). "Then came W. C. Fields, eccentric juggler, in his amusing turn."

57. May 19, 1900. Orpheum Theatre (Omaha, Nebraska). "W. C. Fields, eccentric juggler."

58. June 2, 1900. Empire Theatre (Cleveland, Ohio). "W. C. Fields played the Empire, Cleveland last week. . . . This week at Moore's Wonderland, Detroit, with Shea's, Buffalo, the Chicago Opera House, Ferris Wheel Park and Masonic Temple to follow. He has just closed seven weeks on the Orpheum Circuit."

59. June 9, 1900. Garden Theatre, M. Shea, manager (Buffalo, New York). "Week of June 4, W. C. Fields."

60. June 16, 1900. Koster and Bial's (New York City). "Wm. C. Fields, in his eccentric juggling act, won well deserved approval for his work."

61. June 23, 1900. Koster and Bial's (New York City). "W. C. Fields, juggler. . . .

62. June 30, 1900. "Wm C. Fields opened at Koster and Bial's June

11, and was reengaged after his first performance for another week. He [will play] the Chicago Opera House, June 25; Ferris Wheel Park, July 1; Masonic Temple, July 15; San Souci Park, [July] 22; and Robinson Park, Ft. Wayne, Ind., [July] 29."

63. July 7, 1900. "W. C. Fields has received contracts from the Western Manager's Association for nine weeks' work beginning Oct. 22 at the Olympic Theatre, Chicago." Ferris Wheel Park (Chicago, Illinois). "W. C. Fields, juggler. . . ."

64. July 21, 1900. Masonic Temple Roof Theatre (Chicago, Illinois). "W. C. Fields. . . ."

65. July 28, 1900. San Souci Park (Chicago, Illinois). "W. C. Fields. . . ."

66. Aug. 25, 1900. Keith's Union Square Theatre (New York City). "The week of 20–25. . . . W. C. Fields, a clever tramp juggler."

67. Sept. 1, 1900. Keith's Theatre, George E. Bogle, resident manager (Philadelphia, Pennsylvania). "W. C. Fields."

68. Sept. 8, 1900. Keith's Theatre (Boston, Massachusetts). "W. C. Fields."

69. Sept. 15, 1900. "W. C. Fields is on a tour of the Keith circuit, with Moore's circuit, the Empire, Toledo; Columbus, Cincinnati; Castle's circuit, Columbia, St. Louis and the Orpheum circuits to follow. He opens at the Winter Garden [*sic*], Berlin, Ger., Jan. 1."

70. Sept. 16, 1900. Keith's New Theatre (Providence, Rhode Island). "The programme, 10–13, will include: W. C. Fields. . . ."

71. Sept. 29, 1900. Wonderland Theatre and Musee (Detroit, Michigan). "W. C. Fields, juggler. . . ."

72. Oct. 27, 1900. Olympic Theatre (Chicago, Illinois). "W. C. Fields."

73. Nov. 3, 1900. Haymarket (Chicago, Illinois). "W. C. Fields."

74. Nov. 17, 1900. Chicago Opera House (Chicago, Illinois). "W. C. Fields."

75. Nov. 24, 1900. "W. C. Fields sails on December 12 for Berlin, Germany, to open at the Winter Garden [*sic*], Jan. 1."

76. Jan. 26, 1901. "W. C. Fields wrote that he opened at the Wintergarten, Berlin, Germany, January 1, and was a success. He moved down the bill after the first night seven to twelve. The management tried to prolong the engagement for a second month but could not as other bookings interfered."

77. Feb. 2, 1901. "Our European Letter from our special correspondent. . . . The Wintergarten had Otero as an extra for New Year's Eve . . . W. C. Fields made a terrific hit, and they would not let him off before he had responded to several encores."

While in England, Fields became acquainted with Percy T. Tibbles (1881–1938), a magician, and author of The Magician's Handbook. *Fields provided biographical data, a photo of himself in costume, and an article entitled "New Juggling Tricks" in which he described and illustrated "A New Hat and Cigar Effect" and "The Great Cigar Box Trick." Tibbles wrote, "Unlike the majority of jugglers, Fields did not spend half his life practicing from morning till night until he excelled all others. He liked a juggling show he once saw, and made up his mind to do a similar turn, practicing with that object in view for just one year before he starred as an eccentric juggler at the leading halls of New York" (122).*

78. Fields returned from Europe October, 1901, and toured the United States until his departure from San Francisco in April, 1903, on his first world tour. He returned from his world tour in July, 1905.

79. Aug. 28, 1905. New York Theatre. Klaw & Erlanger's *The Ham Tree* (1905-6 season) 90 performances. Fields' role: Sherlock Baffles.

80. Fields remained with *The Ham Tree* through the 1906-7 season. The first San Francisco production opened at the Novelty Theatre. Jan. 12, 1907, the *San Francisco News Letter* reported that Fields performance was excellent.

THE TIVOLI

Proprietors ... ... TIVOLI Co., Ltd.
Manager ... ... EDWARD A. PICKERING.

Wednesday, February 3rd, 1904.

GRAND NEW COMPANY.

UNPARALLELED ATTRACTIONS.

W. C. FIELDS.

HAYDAS TROUPE.

The SISTERS FLEXMORE.

Miss NINA CARLTON.

BERT: BRANTFORD.

THE SALVAGGIS.

THE BIOSCOPE. | Miss Vivian Dell.

Miss

PEGGY PRYDE.

FAMILY MATINEE EVERY SATURDAY.

NO SMOKING.
LIGHT REFRESHMENTS ONLY.

BOX STALLS, 3s. ORCHESTRA STALLS, 5s. BOXES, £2 2s.
Children, Half-Price.

Doors open 7.30. Commence 7.50 sharp. Carriages at 10.45. Telephone No. 992.

STABLEFORD, LTD. PRINTERS, CAPE TOWN.

Handbill (31.5cm × 20.3cm). Author's collection.

81. May 28, 1907. The *New York Transcript* reported that Fields was appearing at the Jardin de Paris [roof of the New York Theatre].

82. April 23, 1908. *Variety* reported that Fields was going to Europe. He departed from New York on his second European tour, May 1908, and, according to the *New York Star* was back in the United States on December 19, 1908. June, 1910, he began his third European tour.

83. April 27, 1912. The *New York Star* reported that Fields had returned from "a year of tremendous success in England," and was "currently playing the Percy G. Williams Greater New York Circuit."

84. Feb. 10, 1913. Fields played Hammerstein's Victoria Theatre for the first time. During the week of May 10, 1913, he played Keith's Palace Theatre, and for the first time was on the same bill as Sarah Bernhardt.[5]

85. Fields departed from New York on his last world tour in June 1913. By July 11th he was in London, and for the second time, he performed on a bill with Sarah Bernhardt.

86. Oct. 11, 1913. Fields appeared at the London Coliseum in a special performance under Royal patronage. Though not a command performance, he was the only American invited to appear. It was called "The Good Samaritan Performance," and was arranged by Sarah Bernhardt and Lord Lonsdale.[6] This was Fields' third and final performance with Sarah Bernhardt.

Fields ended his last tour in October 1914. Robert Lewis Taylor wrote that Fields sailed from Sydney, Australia, to San Francisco on an American tramp steamer (146). Unfortunately, a fire in 1940 destroyed all passenger lists and arrival records for that period. Therefore, the exact dates must be estimated.

87. Nov. 26, 1914. Empire Theatre. (Syracuse, New York). Charles Dillingham's *Watch Your Step.* (W. C. Fields played one performance.)

88. June 12, 1915. New Amsterdam Theatre (New York). *Ziegfeld Follies* (1915-16 season), 104 performances. Act I, Scene 9—"Some Midnight Cabaret." WCF character: A pool player (with Ed Wynn). Act II, Scene 2—"Home of the Sun." WCF as himself. Act II, Scene 3—"Hallway of the Bunkem Court Apartments." WCF character: Adam Fargo.

89. Sept. 19, 1915. Gaumont. *Pool Sharks.* (First silent film.)

90. Oct. 3, 1915. Gaumont. *His Lordship's Dilemma.*

91. June 12, 1916. New Amsterdam Theatre (New York). *Ziegfeld Follies* (1916-17 season), 112 performances. Act I, Scene 10—"Recruiting." WCF character: Reddan Greene. Act II, Scene 1—"The Blushing Ballet—Travesty of Scheherazade." WCF character: O. Shaw. Act II, Scene 4—"Puck's Pictorial Palace." WCF characters: Josephus Daniels and Teddy Roosevelt. Act II, Scene 5—"A Croquet Game: On the Lawn of Lallypoosa." WCF character: Mr. Zipp, a croquet player.

92. June 12, 1917. New Amsterdam Theatre (New York). *Ziegfeld Follies* (1917-18 season), 111 performances. Act I, Scene 5—"The Episode of the Tennis Match." WCF character: Rufus Racket. Act II, Scene 6—"The Episode of New York Streets and Subway." WCF character: Wise Acres, the peanut man.

93. June 18, 1918. New Amsterdam Theatre (New York). *Ziegfeld Follies* (1918-19 season), 151 performances. Act I, Scene 4—"A Patent Attorney's Office." WCF character: Bunkus Munyan, a patent attorney. Act II, Scene 13—"The Lower Regions." WCF character: Senator La Follette.

94. Fields did not appear in the regular edition of the *Ziegfeld Follies* (1919-20 season). October 26, 1919, he did appear in Ziegfeld's *Tonight at 8:10* Sunday concerts, and in the eighth edition of the *Midnight Frolic.*[7]

95. Dec. 21, 1919. Keith's Hippodrome (New York). Fields participated in the *New York American*'s "Christmas Fund Show."[8]

96. March 15, 1920. New Amsterdam Theatre Roof (New York). *Ziegfeld Danse de Follies:* Midnight Frolic. Part I, Scene 5—"Don't You Remember Me?" Song by Fannie Brice and Messrs. John Price Jones, Thomas Handers, Arthur Milliss and W. C. Fields. Part I, Scene 10—"An Ante-Bellum Diversion." WCF as himself, assisted by Miss Jessie Reed, Mr. John Price Jones, and Mr. William Blanche. Part II, Scene 10—Specialty by Mr. W. C. Fields, assisted by William Blanche. Part III, Scene 6—"Shimmy Homestead." WCF character: The Father.

97. June 22, 1920. New Amsterdam Theatre (New York). *Ziegfeld Follies* (1920-21 season), 123 performances. Act I, Scene 10—"The Family Ford." WCF character: Mr. Fliverton. Act II, Scene 1—"The Little Follies Theatre during the Intermission." W. C. Fields and Fannie Brice.

98. June 21, 1921. Globe Theatre (New York). *Ziegfeld Follies* (1921-22 season), 119 performances. Act I, Scene 4—"The Professor." WCF character: The Deacon. Act I, Scene 14—"Lionel, Ethel and Jack, with Camille Burlesque." WCF character: Jack. Act I, Scene 16—"The Championship of the World." WCF character: The Referee. Act II, Scene 1—"The Birthday of the Dauphin." WCF character: An Old Roue (M. le Duc Chateau Briand). Act II, Scene 5—"The Subway—Off to the Country." WCF character: Mr. Fliverton.

99. March 10, 1922. Agent Billy Grady advertised in *Variety* that W. C. Fields would perform "The Family Ford" at B. F. Keith's Palace, New York City, the week of March 6th; and at Keith's Royal, New York City, the week of March 13th.

100. June 21, 1922. Globe Theatre (New York). *George White Scandals* (4th edition), 88 performances. Act I, Scene 4—"Terrific Traffic." W. C. Fields, Winnie Lightner, Olive Vaughn, Franklyn Ardelle, and Arthur Brooks. Act I, Scene 10—"The Big Leaguers." W. C. Fields, Franklyn Ardelle, Arthur Brooks. Act II, Scene 2—"W. C. Fields Specialty." Act II, Scene 6—"The Radio Bug." W. C. Fields, Colletta Ryan, Winnie Lightner.

101. Sept. 23, 1923. New Apollo Theatre (New York). Philip Goodman's *Poppy*. (1923-24 season), 346 performances. Fields role: Professor Eustace McGargle.

102. Oct. 27, 1924. Hearst Cosmopolitan Pictures. *Janice Meredith.*

103. The *New York Times* reported on December 24, 1924, that Fields would participate in an all "All Star Bill" benefit performance for Willie Gibson at the New Apollo Theatre. Surprisingly, Fields was billed as "*The Comic Supplement*—W. C. Fields & Co." On page eight of the same issue it was reported that "rehearsals for *The Comic Supplement* had just begun a week earlier, and Ziegfeld was still casting for the parts."

Charles Higham wrote that "Ziegfeld made preparations for J. P. McEvoy's *The Comic Supplement* as a vehicle for Fields." He said that "Fields did extensive work on the book after it was purchased from McEvoy by Ziegfeld" (166). The best explanation of how *The Comic Supplement* was reduced from 31 acts to a Ziegfeld revue is given in *Miracle in the Evening*. Norman Bel Geddes wrote, "The answer was simple. All Flo Ziegfeld could understand was his *Follies* formula. A show like *The Comic Supplement* was beyond him. The upshot was that he cut up *The Comic Supplement* and made of the pieces *The Ziegfeld Follies of 1925*" (310).

104. Jan. 20, 1925. National Theatre (Washington, D.C.). *The Comic Supplement.*

105. Jan. 26, 1925. Shubert Theatre (Newark, New Jersey). *The Comic Supplement.* Closed February 14, after a three week run.

106. March 10, 1925. New Amsterdam Theatre (New York). *Ziegfeld Follies* (1925 edition). Dialogue by J. P. McEvoy, Will Rogers, and W. C. Fields. Act I, Scene 3—"The Drug Store." WCF character: Pa. Act I, Scene 7—"A Back Porch." WCF character: Pa. Act II, Scene 5—"The Waltz of Love" by Ray Dooley and W. C. Fields. Act II, Scene 8—"A Road—Joy Ride." WCF character: Pa. Act II, Scene 10—"The Picnic" by J. P. McEvoy and W. C. Fields. Act II, Scene 12—"Play Juror." Will Rogers, W. C. Fields, Martha Lorber.

107. April 25, 1925. Metropolitan Opera House (New York). *Lambs Club Gambol.* Another benefit performance with Fields.

108. May 3, 1925. Keith-Albee Hippodrome (New York). *National Vaudeville Artists Ninth Annual Benefit.* Fields was number 51 on a program of 197 performers.

109. July 6, 1925. New Amsterdam Theatre (New York). *Summer Ziegfeld Follies of 1925*. Dialogue by J. P. McEvoy, Will Rogers, W. C. Fields, and Gus Weinberg. Act I, Scene 3—"The Drug Store." WCF character: Pa. Act I, Scene 6—"A Back Porch." WCF character: Pa. Act II, Scene 3—"A Bedroom. The Nagger—Late into Night, Does Mamma Love Papa?" Characters: The Ball and Chain, Edna Leedom. Her husband, W. C. Fields. Act II, Scene 7—"A Road—Joy Ride." WCF character: Pa. Act II, Scene 9—"The Picnic." WCF character: Pa.

The number of performances was always for the New York run only. Performances for the individual seasons were not recorded because Ziegfeld ran the 19th and 20th editions of the Follies *together. Estimates for the two seasons ranged from 402 to 510 performances, depending upon which theatre reference was consulted.*

110. Aug. 2, 1925. United Artists Corp. *Sally of the Sawdust.*

111. Dec. 7, 1925. Paramount. *That Royale Girl.*

112. May 24, 1926. Paramount. *It's the Old Army Game.*

113. Oct. 25, 1926. Paramount. *So's Your Old Man.*

114. Jan. 31, 1927. Paramount. *The Potters.*

115. Aug. 20, 1927. Paramount. Running Wild.

116. Dec. 17, 1927. Paramount. *Two Flaming Youths.*

117. March 3, 1928. Paramount. *Tillie's Punctured Romance.*

118. May 7, 1928. Paramount. *Fools for Luck.*

119. Aug. 6, 1928. Earl Carroll Theatre (New York). *Earl Carroll Vanities* (7th edition), 203 performances. Dialogue by W. C. Fields and Paul Gerard Smith. Act I, Scene 9—"Stolen Bonds." By W. C. Fields. WCF character: Snavely. Act I, Scene 18—"The Caledonian Express." By W. C. Fields. WCF characters: The Guard, The Conductor, The Station Master, The Policeman (four of the seven characters in the skit). Act I, Scene 22—"All Aboard." By R. T. Tarrant. WCF character: George. Act II, Scene 5—"School Days." By W. C. Fields. WCF character: 3rd Reader. Act II, Scene 9—"The Mormon's Prayer." By Herman Meyer. WCF character: Brigham Young. Act II, Scene 15—"An Episode at the Dentist's." By W. C. Fields. WCF character: Dr. Pain.

120. Nov. 26, 1928. Fields replaced Brian MacDonald as Mr. Hubbard in Act I, Scene 13 of "Mrs. Hubbard's Cupboard."

Fields complained that he worked only 17 weeks in the 1928 Vanities.[9]

121. March 15–16, 1929. Fields was in Florida attending the twin world premiers of the first film version of Edna Ferber's *Showboat.*[10]

122. March 24, 1930. The *New York Times* reported that Fields was heading the bill at the Palace Theatre in "Stolen Bonds" and "Golfing." The *Times* also mentioned that Fields' last appearance at the Palace was eight years earlier (1922), and Fields had a new "Shorty" as caddy in "The Golfer."

123. July 1, 1930. New Amsterdam Theatre (New York). *Earl Carroll Vanities* (8th edition), 215 performances. Fields was not listed as a regular cast member. WCF wrote that he worked only 12 weeks in the *Vanities* that season.

124. Aug. 11, 1930. Municipal Opera Amphitheater. St. Louis, Mo., *Showboat.* Fourteen performances. This was a Milton I. Shubert production with Fields cast as Cap'n Andy. It was also the first American production of *Showboat* not associated with Ziegfeld.[11]

125. Aug. 22, 1930. RKO. Series Title: *Broadway Headliners.* Film Title: *The Golf Specialist.* (Fields' first sound film).

126. Dec. 22, 1930. Hammerstein Theatre (New York). *Ballyhoo* (1930-31 season), 68 performances. Closed the week beginning February 16, 1931. Fields' role: Q. Q. Quayle.

127. Aug. 27, 1931. Earl Carroll Theatre (New York). *Earl Carroll Vanities* (9th edition), 278 performances. Fields was not listed as a regular cast member. Again, WCF wrote that he played only eight weeks that season.

128. Dec. 26, 1931. Warner Brothers-First National. *Her Majesty Love.*

129. July 8, 1932. Paramount. *Million Dollars Legs.*

130. Dec. 2, 1932. Paramount. *If I Had a Million.*

131. Dec. 9, 1932. Paramount. A Mack Sennett Star Comedy. *The Dentist.*

132. March 3, 1933. Paramount. A Mack Sennett Star Comedy. *The Fatal Glass of Beer.*

133. April 21, 1933. Paramount. A Mack Sennett Star Comedy. *The Pharmacist.*

134. May 30, 1933. CBS Radio. *California Melodies.* This was Fields' first guest appearance on radio.[12]

135. June 2, 1933. Paramount. *International House.*

136. June 24, 1933. Vitaphone Corp. Series title: *How to Break Ninety.* Film title: *Hip Action.*

137. July 28, 1933. Paramount. A Mack Sennett Star Comedy. *The Barber Shop.*

138. Sept. 8, 1933. Paramount. *Hollywood on Parade (B-2).*

139. Oct. 13, 1933. Paramount. *Tillie and Gus.*

140. Dec. 22, 1933. Paramount. *Alice in Wonderland.*

141. Feb. 9, 1934. Paramount. *Six of a Kind.*

142. March 17, 1934. CBS Radio. Borden's *Forty-Five Minutes in Hollywood.* Fields' second guest appearance on radio.

143. April 6, 1934. Paramount. *You're Telling Me.*

144. April 27, 1934. Paramount. *Hollywood on Parade (B-10).*

145. July 13, 1934. Paramount. *The Old Fashioned Way.*

146. Oct. 19, 1934. Paramount. *Mrs. Wiggs of the Cabbage Patch.*

147. Nov. 30, 1934. Paramount. *It's a Gift.*

148. Jan. 13, 1935. M-G-M. *David Copperfield.*

149. March 22, 1935. Paramount. *Mississippi.*

150. July 26, 1935. Paramount. *Man on the Flying Trapeze.*

151. June 19, 1936. Paramount. *Poppy.*

152. Jan. 7, 1937. NBC Radio. Program honoring *Adolph Zukor's Silver Jubilee* at Paramount Studio. Fields' portion of the show was broadcast from a hospital bed in Riverside County.

153. March 21, 1937. American Federation of Radio Artists. Fields applied for membership in AFRA.

154. May 17, 1937. NBC News Service announced a contract with W. C. Fields. He was scheduled to appear on the *Chase & Sanborn Hour* with Edgar Bergen and Charlie McCarthy for 16 weeks. Sundays, 8:00 P.M., EDST, NBC-Red Network.

Fields first appeared on the show May 9th, two weeks before the announcement, and was on every Sunday from May 9th through September 26th [21 weeks].[13]

155. Feb. 18, 1938. Paramount. *The Big Broadcast of 1938.*

156. March 7, 1938. CBS Radio. Lux Radio Theater, *Poppy.* Cecil B. DeMille's radio production was broadcast at 6:00 P.M., Pacific Time. Frank Woodruff's report for the J. Walter Thompson Company remarked that "Fields [was] superb and played for radio laughs rather than studio laughs."

157. March 10, 1938. Biltmore Hotel (Los Angeles, California). *Tenth Annual Academy Awards Banquet.* Fields presented a statuette to Mack Sennett "for his lasting contribution to the comedy technique of the screen."[14]

158. May 5, 1938. Paramount Studio. Fields presented a high school diploma to Miss Olymph Bradna. She was the first star ever to be graduated from one of the studio schools. Present at the graduation were Guy M. Hoyt, Los Angeles Board of Education; Rachel Smith, teacher; Baby Leroy, Eugene Zukor, Miss Bradna and Mr. Fields.

159. June 5, 1938. NBC Radio. *Chase & Sanborn Hour.* Fields was a special guest of Bergen and McCarthy.

160. Oct. 15, 1938. CBS Radio. Lucky Strike's *Your Hit Parade.* Fields was featured on this program four times: October 15,

October 22, October 29, and November 5. The show originated from KNX, Los Angeles.

As a writer for *Your Hit Parade,* George Marion created a character for Fields' use in a comedy sketch. The character's name was Larsen E. Whipsnade. Fields liked the name so well he used it in his film *You Can't Cheat an Honest Man.*

161. Dec. 26, 1938. Earl Carroll's *Hollywood Theatre Restaurant.* Fields was a celebrity guest at the grand opening and participated in an all-star number.[15]

162. Feb. 16, 1939. Masquers Club (Hollywood, California). A banquet was given for Fields by friends Gene Fowler, John Barrymore, John Decker, John Carradine, Jack LaRue, et al., to honor his forty plus (41) years in show business.

163. Feb. 17, 1939. Universal. *You Can't Cheat an Honest Man.*

164. March 21, 1939. CBS Radio. *Tuesday Night Party.* Fields special guest appearance.

165. April 23, 1939. CBS Radio. Wrigley's *The Gateway to Hollywood.* Fields guest appearance, hosted by Jesse Lasky.

166. Feb. 9, 1940. Universal. *My Little Chickadee.*

167. Nov. 29, 1940. Universal. *The Bank Dick.*

168. Sept. 21, 1941. NBC Radio. Chase & Sanborn's *Charlie McCarthy Show.* Fields was a special guest.

169. Oct. 10, 1941. Universal. *Never Give a Sucker an Even Break.*

170. June 24, 1942. El Capitan Theatre (Hollywood, California). Ken Murray's *Blackouts of 1942* (1st edition). Fields was a surprise guest artist.[16]

171. Oct. 30, 1942. Twentieth Century—Fox. *Tales of Manhattan.* The Fields portion of the script was written by Bill Morrow and Ed Beloin. Fields' sequence was cut before the film was released. The script was issued in six parts lettered Sequence A through F. Fields' work was in Sequence E.[17]

172. Nov. 8, 1942. NBC Radio. Chase & Sanborn's *Charlie McCarthy Show.* Fields appeared as a special guest.

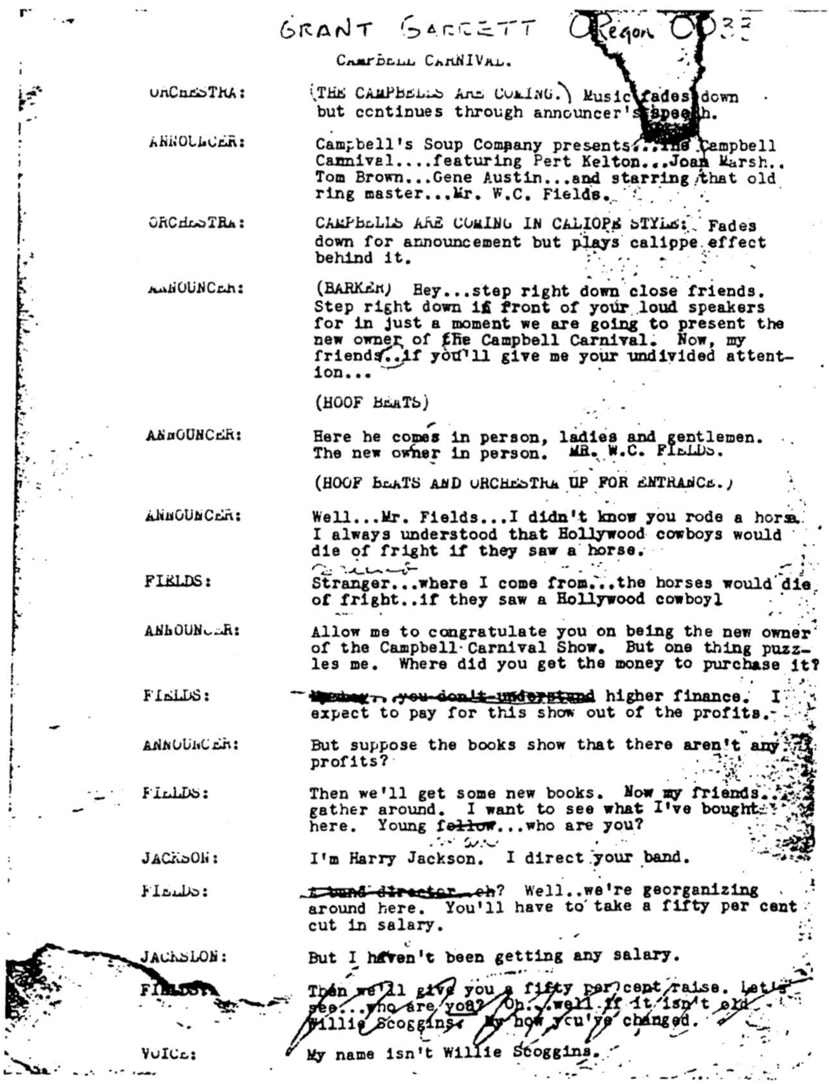

GRANT GARRETT Oregon

CAMPBELL CARNIVAL.

ORCHESTRA: (THE CAMPBELLS ARE COMING.) Music fades down but continues through announcer's speech.

ANNOUNCER: Campbell's Soup Company presents... The Campbell Carnival....featuring Pert Kelton...Joan Marsh.. Tom Brown...Gene Austin...and starring that old ring master...Mr. W.C. Fields.

ORCHESTRA: CAMPBELLS ARE COMING IN CALIOPE STYLE: Fades down for announcement but plays calippe effect behind it.

ANNOUNCER: (BARKER) Hey...step right down close friends. Step right down in front of your loud speakers for in just a moment we are going to present the new owner of the Campbell Carnival. Now, my friends..if you'll give me your undivided attention...

(HOOF BEATS)

ANNOUNCER: Here he comes in person, ladies and gentlemen. The new owner in person. MR. W.C. FIELDS.

(HOOF BEATS AND ORCHESTRA UP FOR ENTRANCE.)

ANNOUNCER: Well...Mr. Fields...I didn't know you rode a horse. I always understood that Hollywood cowboys would die of fright if they saw a horse.

FIELDS: Stranger...where I come from...the horses would die of fright..if they saw a Hollywood cowboy!

ANNOUNCER: Allow me to congratulate you on being the new owner of the Campbell Carnival Show. But one thing puzzles me. Where did you get the money to purchase it?

FIELDS: ~~Monkey.., you don't understand~~ higher finance. I expect to pay for this show out of the profits.

ANNOUNCER: But suppose the books show that there aren't any profits?

FIELDS: Then we'll get some new books. Now my friends.. gather around. I want to see what I've bought here. Young ~~fellow~~...who are you?

JACKSON: I'm Harry Jackson. I direct your band.

FIELDS: ~~A band director, eh~~? Well..we're georganizing around here. You'll have to take a fifty per cent cut in salary.

JACKSON: But I haven't been getting any salary.

FIELDS: Then we'll give you a fifty per cent raise. Let's see...who are you? Oh...well if it isn't old Willie Scoggins. My how you've changed.

VOICE: My name isn't Willie Scoggins.

Radio script (circa 1944). Courtesy Will Fowler collection.

173. Sept. 19, 1943. NBC Radio. Chase & Sanborn's *Charlie McCarthy Show.* Fields was a special guest.

174. NBC Radio. Chase & Sanborn's *Charlie McCarthy Show.* Fields' segment of this show was rebroadcast for Armed

Forces Radio Service in 1945, and again for Chase & Sanborn's 100th Anniversary show in 1964.

175. March 26, 1944. NBC Radio. Chase & Sanborn's *Charlie McCarthy Show.* Fields was a special guest.

176. May 5, 1944. Universal. *Follow the Boys.*

177. June 21, 1944. United Artists. *Song of the Open Road.*

178. June 30, 1944. United Artists. *Sensations of 1945.*

179. Dec. 25, 1944. Armed Forces Radio Service. *Command Performance.* 1944 Christmas Special with Fields.

180. Oct. 28, 1945. CBS Radio. Campbell Soups *Request Performance.* This was the original broadcast of Bill Morrow's "The Temperance Lecture" and "The Day I Drank a Glass of Water" written for Fields.

181. March 24, 1946. NBC Radio Chase & Sanborn's *Charlie McCarthy Show.* Broadcast from the Pasadena Playhouse and included Bergen and McCarthy's visit to Fields at Las Encinas Sanitarium.

182. June 17, 1946. Variety Records. Fields signed a contract to release a 78-rpm album of his broadcast on *Request Performance.*

183. Dec. 25, 1946. Pasadena, California [Wednesday]. W. C. Fields died at 66.

Works Cited

1. James Smart. *W. C. Fields in Philadelphia.* Philadelphia: Shackamaxon Society, Inc., c1972. p. 12. Smart wrote that Fields' performance took place on June 13, 1897, "Friday the 13th." June 13, 1897 was a Sunday. The correct date was May 13, 1898.

2. Bernard Sobel. *Burleycue: An Underground History of Burlesque Days.* New York: Farrar & Rinehart, Inc., c1931. pp. 116–118. Fields' statements to Sobel were verified in the *New York Clipper.*

3. Robert Lewis Taylor. *W. C. Fields: His Follies and Fortunes.* New York: Doubleday & Co., 1949. pp. 47–48. Fields confirmed the year 1898 when he related this incident to Bernard Sobel (Sobel 118).

4. Donald Deschner. *The Films of W. C. Fields.* New York: Citadel

Press, c1966. p. 184. The Irwin's Burlesquers juggling poster of Fields is the earliest known poster in his career.

5. Marion Spitzer. *The Palace.* New York: Atheneum, 1969. p. 23. Copy of program handbill on endpapers.

6. Leslie Carson, ed. *The Stage Year Book 1914.* London: Stage Year Book, 1914. pp. 50–51.

7. Charles Higham. *Ziegfeld.* Chicago: Henry Regnery Co., 1972. pp. 134, 166.

8. "Christmas Fund Show." *New York Times* VIII (21 Dec. 1919), 6:3.

9. Ronald J. Fields. *W. C. Fields by Himself.* New Jersey: Prentice-Hall, c1973. pp. 76, 140.

10. Miles Kreuger. *Showboat: The Story of a Classic American Musical.* New York: Oxford Univ. Press, 1977, p. 84.

11. ________. *Ibid.*, pp. 75, 221.

12. John Behrens. *Letter to author,* dated March 29, 1983. Behrens was Program Information Manager for CBS Broadcast Group.

13. Ted Joyce. *Inventory* of Fields' personal collection of radio transcription disks. 11 pp.

14. James Agee. "Comedy's Greatest Era." *Life* 27-10 (5 Sept. 1949): 70–82, 85–86, 88. Photo of Fields, Frank Capra, and Mack Sennett at 1938 Academy Awards.

15. Ken Murray. *The Body Merchant: The Story of Earl Carroll.* Pasadena: Ward Ritchie Press, c1976. p. 210.

16. ________. *Life on a Pogo Stick. Autobiography of a Comedian.* New York: Holt, Rinehart & Winston, c1960. p. 85, and photo facing p. 116.

17. Complete copy of *script* in author's collection.

BIBLIOGRAPHY

Books, Catalogs, Pamphlets

184. Academy of Motion Picture Arts and Sciences. *W. C. Fields: A Centennial Tribute.* January 29, 1980. [Beverly Hills]: Academy Foundation, 1980. 21*l.* [2].

Typescript of speeches honoring Fields with two page program of his films and a U.S. Postal Service "First Day of Issue" cover in envelope.

185. Adrian, Werner. *Speed Cinema of Motion.* New York: Bounty Books, c1975. p. 110, [1].

WCF on pages 81–82. Photo from *Never Give a Sucker an Even Break.*

186. Agee, James. *Agee on Film: Reviews and Comments.* Boston: Beacon Press, 1958. 432 pp.

WCF on pages 4, 16–17, 26, 235, 334–335, 345.

187. Allen, Steve. *The Funny Men.* New York: Simon & Schuster, 1956. 279pp.

WCF on pages 3–4, 60, 62, 78, 123–124.

188. Amory, Cleveland and Frederic Bradlee. ed. *Vanity Fair: A Cavalcade of the 1920's and 1930's. Selections from America's Most Memorable Magazine.* New York: Viking Press, 1960. 327pp.

WCF on pages 81–82, 103.

189. Anderson, Janice. *History of Movie Comedy.* New York: Exeter Books, 1985. 191pp.

WCF on pages 63–66, 80, 85.

190. Andrews, Robert D. *If I Had a Million: Movie Title of Windfall.* With scenes from the Paramount Picture. New York: Grosset & Dunlap, c1931. 280pp.

Photoplay edition. Four photos: one facing title page, one facing p. 80, one facing p. 144, and one facing p. 208 [WCF scene].

191. Anger, Kenneth. *Kenneth Anger's Hollywood Babylon II.* New York: Plume Printing, 1985. pp. 331, [1].
Reprint of E. P. Dutton's 1984 edition. WCF on pages 170–171, 218, 273. Has WCF x-rated booklet on page 273.

192. Baer, "Bugs" [Arthur] and Henry Major. *Hollywood with "Bugs" Baer and Henry Major.* [Hollywood]: Daniel Murphy & Co., Inc., c1938. [130]pp. Limited to 800 copies.
Has full page pencil sketch of Fields by Henry Major with caption by "Bugs" Baer.

193. Barris, George and Jack Scagnetti. *Cars of the Stars.* New York: Jonathan David Publishers, c1974. 254 pp.
Page 99, photo of Fields' 1932 V-16 Cord.

194. Barry, Iris. *Let's Go to the Movies.* New York: Payson & Clarke Ltd., 1926. 278pp.
WCF on pages 138, 224.

195. Beck, Jerry and Will Friedwald. *Looney Tunes and Merrie Melodies: A Complete Illustrated Guide to the Warner Bros. Cartoons.* New York: Henry Holt & Co., Inc., c1989. pp. 385, [5].
WCF cartoons on pages 40, 49, 51, 53, 65, 69, 73, 76, 105, 111.

196. Bel Geddes, Norman. *Miracle in the Evening. An Autobiography . . .* edited by William Kelley. New York: Doubleday & Co., 1960. 352pp.
WCF on pages 305–312.

197. Bergman, Andrew. *We're in the Money: Depression America and Its Films.* New York: New York University Press, 1971. 200pp.
WCF on pages 30, 33, 38, 41, 55, 60.

198. Blum, Daniel C. *A Pictorial History of the American Theatre, 1860–1960.* New York: Chilton, 1960. 384pp.
WCF on pages 91–92, 156, 161, 167, 171, 179, 188, 194, 195, 205–207, 239.

199. Bohm, H. L. *The Big Broadcast of 1938: W. C. Fields.* London: Becolor Ltd., n.d. [16]pp.
Series: Cinegram No. 30.

200. Boller, Jr., Paul F. and Ronald L. Davis. *Hollywood Anecdotes.* New York: William Morrow & Co., c1987. pp. 493 [1].
WCF on pages 145, 242–244, 255–257, 296, 328, 421.

201. Bordman, Gerald. *American Musical Theatre: A Chronicle.* New York: Oxford University Press, 1978. 749pp.
WCF on pages 212, 307, 322, 333, 350, 363, 372, 380, 389, 414, 440, 462, 466, 477.

202. Buxton, Frank and Bill Owen. *The Big Broadcast, 1920–1950.* A new, revised, and greatly expanded edition of *Radio's Golden Age,* the complete reference work. New York: Viking Press, [1972]. 392pp.
WCF on pages 97, 339.

203. Byron, Stuart and Elisabeth Weis. ed. *The National Society of Film Critics on Movie Comedy.* New York: Grossman Publishers, 1977, 308pp.
WCF on pages 3, 21, 23–24, 37, 41, 49–52, 53, 54, 120, 123–124, 225.

204. Cahn, William. *A Pictorial History of the Great Comedians.* New York: Grosset & Dunlap, Inc., c1975. 224pp. WCF on pages 9, 63, 65, 67, 77–81, 82, 97, 127, 131, 146, 149, 153, 219.
Originally published as *The Laugh Makers: A Pictorial History of American Comedians.* New York: Putnam, 1957. 192pp. WCF on pages 77–81.

205. Cantor, Eddie. *As I Remember Them.* New York: Duell, Sloan and Pearce, c1963. 144pp.
WCF on pages 24, 29–32, 37, 49, 56, 111, 139.

206. ________. *My Life Is in Your Hands.* New York: Blue Ribbon Books, 1932. 309pp.
Reprint of Harper's 1928 edition. WCF on pages 195–199.

207. ________. *Take My Life.* New York: Doubleday & Co., 1957. 288pp.
WCF: Chapter 13.

208. Carnegie, Dale. *Five Minute Biographies.* New York: Southern Publishers, 1937. 256pp.
WCF on pages 169–174.

209. Carroll, Lewis [pseud]. *Alice's Adventures in Wonderland and Through the Looking Glass* (Complete in One Volume). . . . With specially posed illustrations from the Paramount Photoplay. New York: Grosset & Dunlap, n.d. [1933]. pp. 297, [1].
Contains 32 photos. 16 photos on front and rear endpapers, and 16 within the text. Photo opposite title page and photos opposite pages 34, 50, 66, 82, 98, 114, 130, 146, 162, 178, 194, 210, 226, 242, 258. Charlotte Henry photo on dust jacket.

210. ________. *Song Folio of Paramount's "Alice in Wonderland."* Original lyrics by Lewis Carroll. Music by Dimitri Tiomkin and Nathaniel Finston. New York: DeSylva, Brown, and Henderson, Inc., 1933. 32pp.
Front and rear covers illustrated with 20 photos; 4 photos in text with 12 songs. Has table of contents and cast of characters.

211. Carson, L., ed. *"The Stage" Year Book.* London: "The Stage," 1914. 342pp. [For the year 1913].
WCF on pages *l*, 51; photos between pages 56–57.

212. Carter, Randolph. *The World of Flo Ziegfeld.* New York: Praeger Publishers, c1974. 176pp.
WCF on pages 55, 63–65, 82, 85, 127, 130, 171–172. Has three photos of Fields; Appendix records his Follies appearances.

213. Cerf, Bennett. *An Encyclopedia of Modern American Humor.* New York: Doubleday, 1954. 688pp.
Fields vs. McCarthy radio script on pages 525–527.

214. ________. *Try and Stop Me.* New York: Simon & Schuster, 1944. 378pp.
WCF on pages 50–52, 97.

215. [Charrière, Jacques. ed]. *Anthologie du Cinéma.* Paris: L'Avant-Scène-C.I.B., 1966–70. 5v. pp. 557, 574, 542, 566, 566.

Revised and expanded edition. v. 4, WCF material by Jean-Pierre Coursodon on pages 49–112. First edition, 1946–1950. Editor, Marcel La Pierre.

216. Chevalier, Maurice. *Ma Route et Mes Chansons: Londres, Hollywood, Paris.* Paris: René Julliard, 1948. v. 2, 241pp. [Nine volume set].
WCF on pages 134, 222–223.

217. Christie's East. *Collectibles.* Thursday, December 14, 1989, at 10:00 A.M. and 2:00 P.M. . . . New York: Christie's East, 1989. [104]pp.
WCF on front cover, and pages 90–98. Property of Ginger Michael. The Magda Michael Archive of W. C. Fields Material. Four Parts: I. Manuscripts and handwritten material, 21 lots. II. Typescripts and mimeoscripts, 14 lots. III. Correspondence, 19 lots. IV. Various Fields memorabilia, 12 lots. Catalog has eight photo illustrations.

218. Churchill, Allen. *The Great White Way. A Re-creation of Broadway's Golden Era of Theatrical Entertainment.* Illustrated. New York: E. P. Dutton & Co., 1962. 310pp.
WCF on pages [210], 261–262, 288.

219. ________. *Remember When.* [1900–1942]. New York: Golden Press, c1967. pp. 287, [1].
WCF on pages 124, 130, 245.

220. ________. *The Theatrical 20's.* New York: McGraw-Hill Book Co., c1975. 326pp.
WCF on pages 24, 48, 50, 74, 76, 80, 90, 93, 97–98, 193, 259, 284, 312.

221. Committee on Scripts for Soldier and Sailor Shows of the Writer's War Board. *Volume IX (Comedy Sketch Book No. 2)* Abbott & Costello, Burns & Allen, Fred Allen, Charlie McCarthy, Fibber McGee & Molly; Comedy Scenes. Washington, D.C.: The Infantry Journal, Inc., 1943. 128pp.
WCF on pages 25–29. "Insult Spot" radio script distributed by the Special Services Division, A.S.F. "For use exclusively in Military and Naval Establishments by personnel of the Armed Forces of the United States."

222. Corio, Ann. *This Was Burlesque* with Joseph DiMona. New York: Grosset & Dunlap, c1968. 207pp.
Castle Books, Inc., edition. WCF on pages 39–40, 42–46, 62–64, 68, 108. Includes early Fields photo.

223. Coursodon, Jean-Pierre. *W. C. Fields 1879–1946.* Paris: L'Avant-Scène du Cinema, 1968. [64]pp.
Pages 48–112 of v. 4, *Anthologie du Cinema.* Signatures bound separately as No. 32 in a series of booklets [February, 1968].

224. Cowie, Peter. ed. *Hollywood 1920–1970.* New York: A. S. Barnes & Co., c1977. 286pp.
WCF on pages [26], 51, 66, 87, [89], 105, 166.

225. Crist, Judith. *The Private Eye, The Cowboy, and The Very Naked Girl. Movies from Cleo to Clyde.* New York: Holt, Rinehart, and Winston, c1967-68. 292pp.
WCF on pages 32, 107, 225–228.

226. [Crosby, Harry L.]. *Call Me Lucky* by Bing Crosby as told to Pete Martin. New York: Simon & Schuster, 1953. 344pp.
WCF on pages 155–156 (includes photo).

227. Croy, Homer. *Star Maker: The Story of D. W. Griffith.* New York: Duell, Sloan and Pearce, c1959. 210pp.
WCF on pages iii, viii, 168–169, 180, 195, 201.

228. Denebrink, Joyce. ed. *Barbed Wires: A Collection of Famous Funny Telegrams.* New York: Simon & Schuster, c1965. [125]pp.
Charley Mack's telegram to Fields with reply.

229. Deschner, Donald. *The Films of W. C. Fields.* New York: Citadel Press, c1966. 192pp.
First publication of a Fields filmography. Illustrated with photo's [page 22, photo in lower left should read: From the *Comic Supplement,* 1925; page 23, Fields was not in the 1922 Follies].

230. Dickens, Charles. *The Personal History of David Copperfield.* Illustrated with scenes from the Metro-Goldwyn-Mayer Picture. New York: Dodd, Mead & Co., 1935. 850pp.
Series: The International Classics. Has 16 photos and the cast of characters from the movie.

231. ________. *The Personal History of David Copperfield.* New York: Grosset & Dunlap, n.d. [1935]. 881pp.

Series: Universal Library. Dust jacket illustrated with WCF and cast members. Book illustrated with six line drawings from the movie scenes: frontispiece, facing pages 180, 340, 500, 660, 820. WCF facing page 340.

232. ________. *David Copperfield.* Film version by MGM. Story retold and edited by C. M. Martin (MA, Oxon). Woodchester, Stroud, Glos.: Arthurs Press Ltd., [1935]. 64pp.

Souvenir Series No. 1. 45 photos. Illustrated covers.

233. ________. *David Copperfield.* Retold by Eleanor Packer and illustrated with scenes from the Metro-Goldwyn-Mayer Production starring W. C. Fields, . . . Racine, Wisconsin: Whitman Publishing Co., c1934. pp. 156 [2].

A Big Little Book, #1148. Illustrated covers and 76 black & white photos.

234. ________. *David Copperfield.* Illustrierten Filmkurier Nr. 1287. Wien: Eigentümer, Herausgber und Verieger Filmpropaganda Gen. m. b. H., [1935]. [8]pp.

[Wien = Vienna]. 8 pages photos.

235. Disney, Walter. *Mickey's Magic Hat and The Cookie Carnival* with pictures by Walt Disney. Racine, Wisconsin: Whitman Publishing Co., c1937. 24pp.

WCF caricature, Old Man Red Beak, on pages 8–9. Cover title: *Walt Disney's Silly Symphony, Mickey's Magic Hat and The Cookie Carnival.*

236. Durgnat, Raymond. *The Crazy Mirror: Hollywood Comedy and the American Image.* London: Faber & Faber, Ltd., c1969. 280pp.

WCF on pages 92, 142–148, 152, 171, 175, 214, 233, 247, 253.

237. Eames, John Douglas. *The MGM Story: The Complete History of Fifty-Seven Roaring Years.* New York: Crown Publishers, Inc., 1985. 408pp.

Second revised edition, 1982; reprinted 1985. WCF on pages 12, 100, 107, 218.

238. ________. *The Paramount Story.* New York: Crown Publishers, Inc., c1985. 368pp.

WCF on pages 33, 37, 43–45, 51, 59, 85–86, 91, 96, 99, 104–106, 108, 111, 121, 125, 131, 163, 316, 333.

239. Eastman, Max. *Enjoyment of Laughter.* New York: Simon & Schuster, 1936. 366pp.

WCF on pages 69, 91–94, 150, 279, 294, 296–297, 336.

240. Edelson, Edward. *Funny Men of the Movies.* New York: Doubleday & Co., 1976. 127pp.

WCF on pages 24–25, 71–79, 80, 85, 92, 94, 99, 121.

241. Edmonds, I. G. and Reiko Mimura. *Paramount Pictures and the People Who Made Them.* New York: A. S. Barnes & Co., c1980. 272pp.

WCF on pages 125, 127, 137, 139, 155, 198, 200, 210, 216.

242. Everson, William K. *The Art of W. C. Fields.* New York: Bobbs-Merrill Co., c1967. 232 pp.

Illustrated with photos. Not indexed.

243. Ewen, David. *Complete Book of the American Musical Theater.* Revised. A Guide to more than 300 productions of the American Musical Theater from The Black Crook (1866) to the Present, with plot, production, history, stars, songs, composers, librettists, and lyricists, illustrated with photographs. New York: Henry Holt & Co., c1959. 455pp.

WCF on pages 48, 140, 162–163, 172, 299, 362, 369. First edition, 1958. WCF on pages 21–22, 121, 144–146, 155, 290, 357, 365.

244. Farnsworth, Marjorie. *The Ziegfeld Follies.* New York: Putnam, 1956. 194pp.

WCF on pages 50, 73, 77–80, 149.

245. Ferguson, Otis. *The Film Criticism of Otis Ferguson.* Edited by Robert Wilson. Philadelphia: Temple University Press, 1971. 475pp.

WCF on pages 22–23, 36–37, 66, 78, 87–89, 113, 183, 323, 326–327, 395–396, 400.

246. Fields, Ronald J. *W. C. Fields: A Life on Film.* New York: St. Martin's Press, c1984. 256pp.

Contains data not in Deschner's filmography. Opinions and conclusions in the commentary are not always valid. *Million Dollar Legs,* song title is "It's Terrific," not "When I Get Hot in Klopstockia."

247. Fields, W. C. *W. C. Fields by Himself: His Intended Autobiography.* Commentary by Ronald J. Fields. Englewood Cliffs, New Jersey: Prentice-Hall, c1973. 510pp.

Contains previously unpublished drawings, letters, notes, radio scripts, typescripts, articles, and photos of Fields. Except for the commentary, this is the most important Fields book.

248. ________. *Drat! Being the Encapsulated View of Life by W. C. Fields in His Own Words.* Edited by Richard J. Anobile. New York: World Publishing Co., c1968. 128pp.

Contains a reprint of Fields' autobiographical article "From Boy Juggler to Star Comedian," first published in *Theater,* October 1928.

249. ________. *Fields for President.* Drawings by O. Soglow. New York: Dodd, Mead & Co., 1940. 120pp.

Five of the eight chapters in the book appeared in *This Week* magazine, 1938–1941. Chapters "How to Make New Year's Resolutions," and "How to Figure Your Income Tax" were retitled when the book was published.

250. ________. *Fields for President.* Illustrated with photographs. Commentary and photograph selection by Michael M. Taylor. New York: Dodd, Mead & Co., c1971. 163pp.

Reprint with photos from Fields' films.

251. ________. *Fields' Day: The Best of W. C. Fields.* Kansas City, Missouri: Hallmark, c1972. [26]pp.

Both covers, plus front and rear end-papers are illustrated. Book has 17 photos and 46 quotations attributed to Fields. Colophon on back cover: Hallmark/Attic Press/175 HE-2.

252. ________. *A Flask of Fields. Verbal & [sic] and Visual Gems from the Films of W. C. Fields.* Edited by Richard J. Anobile. New York: W. W. Norton & Co., c1972. 272pp.

Contains "over 700 sequential frame blow-ups and dialogue taken directly from the original films. . . ."

253. ———. *"Godfrey Daniels!" Verbal and Visual Gems from the Short Films of W. C. Fields.* Edited by Richard J. Anobile. New York: Crown Publishers, c1975. 224pp.
"Over 800 frame blow-ups and dialogue from the short films [Mack Sennett] of W. C. Fields."

254. ———. *I Never Met a Kid I Liked.* Edited by Paul Mason. Los Angeles: Stanyan Books, c1970. [60]pp.
Stanyan Books No. 4. Has illustrated end-papers and 20 photos with Fields quotations.

255. ———. *Never Trust a Man Who Doesn't Drink.* Compiled by Paul Mason. Hollywood: Stanyan Books, c1971. [60]pp.
Stanyan Books, No. 32. Has 14 drawings of Fields by Brian Hijiwara.

256. ———. *The Quotations of W. C. Fields.* Compiled by Martin Lewis. New York: Drake Publishers, c1976. 160pp.
Contains a list of Fields pseudonyms, and a bibliography of seven books. One photo on front cover, and 60 photos within text.

257. ———. *W. C. Fields in the Bank Dick.* New York: Simon & Schuster, c1973. 88pp.
Classic Film Scripts 21635. "All major differences between this version and the final film are described in the notes to the screenplay." Illustrations, ninety notations, and two contemporary reviews of the film.

258. ———. *W. C. Fields in Never Give a Sucker an Even Break and Tillie and Gus.* New York: Simon & Schuster, c1973. 124pp.
Classic Film Scripts 21392. Illustrated.

259. ———. *W. C. Fields Speaks.* Los Angeles: Price/Stern/Sloan Publishers, Inc., 1981. 79pp.
38 photos with quotations, and partial filmography.

260. Fields, W. C., Jr., and Raymond Rohauer. *A Tribute to W. C. Fields.* New York: Gallery of Modern Art, c1967. [8]pp.
Contains an article by W. C. Fields, Jr., and an interview

of Fields, Jr., by Raymond Rohauer. Some of the dates and events are not correctly cited. 18 photos and filmography.

261. Finch, Christopher and Linda Rosenkrantz. *Gone Hollywood.* New York: Doubleday & Co., 1979. 396pp.
WCF on pages 62, 81, 87, 92, 122, 141, 160, 213, 223, 228, 251, 294, 318, 325, 339. Double page photo [pp. 96–97] of the stand-ins of famous stars including John Sinclair (Fields stand-in).

262. Finke, Blythe Foote. *W. C. Fields, Renowned Comedian of the Early Motion Picture Industry.* New York: SamHar Press, 1972. 30pp.
Series: Outstanding personalities no. 48. Bibliography: pp. 29–30.

263. Firestone, Ross. *The Big Radio Comedy Program.* Chicago: Contemporary Books, Inc., c1978. 250pp.
WCF on pages 74–83, 181, 187, 191–196. Includes reprints of the following radio scripts: *The Golf Tournament,* 1937; and *Fire in the Home,* 1939.

264. Fitzgerald, Ed[ward]. *Tales for Males.* n.p.: Cadillac Publishing Co., 1945. 309pp.
Contains reprint of Chapter 2, "My Views on Marriage" from *Fields for President,* pp. 217–222.

265. Florey, Robert. *Hollywood d'Hier et d'Aujourd'hui.* Paris: Editions Prisma, c1948. 381pp.
WCF on pages 39, 247–249.

266. Flythe, Starkey, Jr. ed. *The Saturday Evening Post Movie Book.* Indianapolis, Indiana: Curtis Pub. Co., c1977. pp. 151, [1].
WCF on pages 51, 126. Article by Alva Johnston entitled "Artful Codger," dated 1932. The article refers to Dr. Citron's 1937 suit against Fields which could not have been published in 1932. The photo is from Fields' 1940 film *My Little Chickadee.*

267. Ford, Corey. *The Time of Laughter.* Boston: Little, Brown & Co., 1967. 232pp.
WCF on pages 1–2, 133, 158, 167, 169–170, 171–195, 220.

268. Ford, Paul Leicester. *Janice Meredith.* New York: Grosset & Dunlap, [1924]. 503pp.

Marion Davies edition with eight photos from the film. Although brief, this was Fields' third film appearance. Fields was not pictured in the book, but was listed in the film credits.

269. Fowler, Gene. *Minutes of the Last Meeting.* New York: Viking Press, 1954. 277pp.

John Decker drawings on end-papers. Book was not indexed. WCF on pages [6, 8–10, 22, 24–25, 27, 31, 33, 34, 36–38, 40, 44–49, 55–60, 84, 99–106, 112, 151–155, 160, 169, 171–175, 193–196, 204, 207, 221–228, 230, 234–236, 241, 242, 248, 250–253, 261, 270].

270. Fowler, Will. *The Second Handshake.* Secaucus, New Jersey: Lyle Stuart, Inc., c1980. 301pp.

WCF on pages 11, 15, 24, 25, 49, 64, 65, 89, 95–135, 163–166, 188, 197, 207, 211, 242, 278, [279], 287. Photos between pp. 96–97, pp. 192–193. Fields' Last Will & Testament was reproduced for the first time with newspaper details regarding litigation of his Estate.

271. ________. *The Young Man from Denver.* New York: Doubleday & Co., Inc., 1962. 310pp.

WCF on pages 11, 146, 180, 200, 216–219, 227–228, 230, 236, 249–250, 257, 262, 265, 279, 290–291, 309. Photos are between pages 96–97 and pages 216–217. Fields' photos are numbered 13 and 19.

272. Freeman, Don. *In a Flea's Navel: A Critic's Love Affair with Television.* New York: A. S. Barnes & Co., c1980. 229pp.

WCF on pages [34], 40–41, 52, 82.

273. Gehring, Wes D. *W. C. Fields: A Bio-bibliography.* Westport, Connecticut: Greenwood Press, c1984. 233pp.

Series title: Popular Culture Bio-Bibliographies.

274. Gilbert, Douglas. *American Vaudeville: Its Life and Times.* New York: McGraw-Hill Book Co., Inc., c1940. 428pp.

WCF on pages 8, 269, 270, 273–274, 279.

275. Gilmore, Donald H. *Sex in Comics; A History of the Eight Pagers.*

San Diego: Greenleaf Classics, Inc., 1971. 4v. GP602 v. 1 "The Early Years, 1930–37." 191pp. GP603 v. 2 "Mr. Prolific, King of the Comics." 192pp. GP604 v. 3 "The World's Fair." 208pp. GP605 v. 4 "An Attempt to Expand." 143pp.

WCF in v. 3 on pages 124–125 (Plates 486–494). "Artist No. 9, circa 1939." *She Loved It with Bill Bloome.* [Also issued as *She Loved It with W. C. Fields*].

276. Golden, George Fuller. *My Lady Vaudeville and Her White Rats,* by George Fuller Golden, Founder and First Big Chief of the White Rats of America. New York: Published under the auspices of The Board of Directors of the White Rats of America, 1909. 2pp. 1*l*, ii, 199pp., 49pp. ads, 1*l*,, 13pp. professional cards, 2pp. hotels.

Professional Card: "W. C. Fields, Juggler."

277. Grady, Billy. *The Irish Peacock: The Confessions of a Legendary Talent Agent.* New York: Arlington House, c1972. 299pp.

WCF on pages 10–41, 70, 128, 130, 180, 185, 187, 214–216, 283.

278. Green, Abel and Joe Laurie, Jr. *Show Biz: From Vaude to Video.* New York: Henry Holt, 1951. 613pp.

WCF on pages 26, 39, 80, 163, 178, 259, 294, 550.

279. Green, Stanley. *The Great Clowns of Broadway.* New York: Oxford University Press, 1984. 247pp.

WCF on pages viii, 8, 9, 10, 11, 12, 14, 25, 39, 67–82, 83, 103, 137, 180, 208–211, 240.

280. ________. *The World of Musical Comedy.* The story of the American musical stage told through the careers of its foremost composers and lyricists. . . . Revised and Enlarged Edition. New York: A. S. Barnes & Co., [1986]. 541pp.

WCF on pages 205, 419, 425, 442, 449–450, 453–454.

281. Greene, Grahame. *Grahame Greene on Film: Collected Film Criticism, 1935–1940.* Edited by John Russell Taylor. New York: Simon & Schuster, c1972. 284pp.

WCF on pages 12, 87–88.

282. Griffith, Richard and Arthur Mayer. *The Movies: The Sixty Year History of the World of Hollywood and Its Effect on America,*

from Pre-Nickelodeon Days to the Present. New York: Simon & Schuster, 1957. 442pp.
WCF on pages 299, 313, 316–317, 400.

283. Grunwald, E. A. ed. *Variety Radio Directory, 1937–38.* 1st Annual Edition. n.p.: Variety, Inc., 1937. 1104pp.
WCF on pages 54, 943.

284. Halliwell, Leslie. *The Filmgoer's Companion.* New York: Hill & Wang, 1965. 469pp.
WCF on pages 270–271.

285. ________. *Mountain of Dreams. The Golden Years of Paramount Pictures.* New York: Stonehill Pub. Co., c1976. 196pp.
WCF on pages [x], 36, 48–51, 87, 93, 98, 100, 172. "Every film sold to exhibitors was accompanied by a "campaign book" [*sic*] of publicity material." Book has film advertisements [from press books] for 12 Fields Paramount productions. [Campaign books were sent to exhibitors to announce coming attractions.]

286. Hansen, Al[fred]. *Incomplete Requiem for W. C. Fields.* New York: Great Bear Pamphlet, 1966. [16]pp.
A poem read by the author in an early (1958) "happening" while Fields' movies were projected on his bare chest at the E-pit-o-me Coffe House in Greenwich Village.

287. Harlan, Kenneth and Rex Lease. *What Actors Eat When They Eat.* Los Angeles: Lymanhouse, 1939. 241pp.
Page 90 has a photo of Fields with his recipes for Brandied Peaches, and Omelet Au Rum.

288. Harmon, Jim. *The Great Radio Comedians.* New York: Doubleday & Co., 1970. 195pp.
WCF on pages 9–13, 71, 142, 151, and photo facing p. 76. Includes illustration of an unscripted change in dialogue between Charlie McCarthy and Fields. Special edition containing a 33⅓ rpm record of Fields, and Burns & Allen from their radio programs.

289. Hecht, Andrew. *Hollywood Merry-Go-Round.* Illustrated by Leo Hershfield. Introduction by Bob Hope. New York: Grosset & Dunlap, c1947. 212pp.
WCF on pages 192–193.

290. Henderson, Robert M. *D. W. Griffith: His Life and Work.* New York: Oxford University Press, 1972. 326pp.
WCF on pages 256, 259, 260, [307]. There are two photos of Fields between pages 214–215.

291. Higham, Charles. *Ziegfeld.* Chicago: Henry Regnery Co., c1972. 245pp.
WCF on pages 118, 124, [134], 146, 158–159, 165, 166, 169. [WCF photos between pages 180–181].

292. Hirschhorn, Clive. *The Universal Story.* New York: Crown Publishers, Inc., c1983. 400pp.
WCF on front cover, poster decor facing title page, and pages 97, 98, 112, [113], 116, 118, 126, 146.

293. ________. *The Warner Bros. Story.* New York: Crown Publishers, Inc., c1979. 480pp.
WCF on page 107.

294. Hope, Bob. *The Road to Hollywood: My 40-Year Love Affair with the Movies,* by Bob Hope with Bob Thomas. New York: Doubleday & Company, 1977. 271pp.
WCF on pages 21–23, 119, 122, 123, 164.

295. Jessel, George. *Halo Over Hollywood.* Van Nuys: Toastmaster Publishing Co., c1963. 176pp.
"Anthology of messages from famous Hollywood personalities as might be spoken from the world beyond." WCF on pages 7–9. Caricature and poem.

296. Knight, Arthur. *The Liveliest Art: A Panoramic History of the Movies.* New York: MacMillan, 1957. 383pp.
WCF on pages 37, 172–173, 175, 260.

297. Kreuger, Miles. *Show Boat: The Story of a Classic American Musical.* New York: Oxford University Press, 1977. 246pp.
WCF on pages 75, 84, [221]. First book to document Fields' role as Cap'n Andy in *Show Boat.* Fields was the first Cap'n Andy in a non–Ziegfeld production.

298. Lamparski, Richard. *Lamparski's Hidden Hollywood Where the Stars Lived, Loved, and Died.* New York: A Fireside Book, 1981. 128pp.
WCF on pages 50–51.

299. Leonard, Eddie. *What a Life I'm Telling You.* New York: Published by Eddie Leonard, c1934. pp. 240, [2].

WCF on pages [54, 85–86, 90–92, 105, 113, 115, 149–150, with photos of Fields facing pages 109, 148, 209]. Book is not indexed.

300. Lewine, Harris. *Good-Bye to All That.* New York: McGraw-Hill, c1970. [128]pp.

Cover title: *Flat Seventies Cigarettes, Good-Bye to All That.* Illustrated history of cigarettes in America. WCF on pages 102–103, 122.

301. Longley, M., L. Silverstein, and S. A. Tower. *America's Taste: The Cultural Events of a Century Reported by Contemporary Observers in the Pages of the New York Times 1851–1959.* New York: Simon & Schuster, 1960. 332pp.

WCF on page 173.

302. Longworth, Bertram. *Hold Still Hollywood.* Portraiture, Composite, Photomontage. n.p.: Ivan Deach, Jr., 1937. [116]pp. Limited to 1,000 copies.

WCF photo with caption on page 62.

303. McCaffrey, Donald W. *The Golden Age of Sound Comedy: Comic Figures and Comedians of the Thirties.* New Jersey: A. S. Barnes & Co., c1973. 208pp.

WCF on pages 165–182.

304. McCallum, John. *Scooper: Authorized Story of Scoop Conlon's Motion Picture World.* Seattle: Wood & Reber, Publishers, 1960. 274pp.

WCF on pages [87–95, 103, 105, 106, 109, 139, 204–206, 245, 250, 265, 266. Four photos of Fields between pages 196–197]. Book is not indexed.

305. McLaughlin, John K. *Literature, Art and Artifacts That Will Forever Remain Among the Undead.* The Book Sail 16th Anniversary Catalogue. Edited by Bruce Francis. Orange, California: McLaughlin Press, 1984. [276]pp. Limited to 1400 copies: "All copies have been hand-numbered using an ink compound containing human blood."

A magnificent catalog illustrated by Robert Bloch and Ray Bradbury. WCF part I, Item F. Stage sides from the broadway production of *Poppy* by Dorothy Donnelly, 1923.

306. Maltin, Leonard. *The Great Movie Comedians: From Charlie Chaplin to Woody Allen.* New York: Crown Publishers, 1978. 238pp.
WCF on pages 142, 143–151, 159, 160.

307. ________. *The Great Movie Shorts.* New York: Crown Publishers, Inc., 1972. 236pp.
WCF on pages [x], 19, 80–84, 120, 158, 189, 218.

308. ________. *Of Mice and Magic: A History of American Animated Cartoons.* New York: McGraw-Hill Book Co., c1980. 470pp.
WCF on page 234.

309. Manchel, Frank. *The Talking Clowns: From Laurel and Hardy to the Marx Brothers.* New York: Franklin Watts, 1976. 129pp.
WCF on pages 25–52, 76–78.

310. Marlowe, Don. *The Hollywood That Was.* Fort Worth, Texas: Branch-Smith, Inc., 1969. pp. 189, [3].
WCF on pages [18–20, 27–29, 55, 184]. Not indexed.

311. Marx, Kenneth S. *Star Stats: Who's Whose in Hollywood.* Los Angeles: Price/Stern/Sloan, 1979. 436pp.
Book contains errors. For example: Fields' date of birth is given as February 10, 1879, and Joe E. Brown is listed as Fields' partner.

312. Marx, Samuel. *Broadway Portraits.* New York: Donald Flamm, Inc., 1929. 63pp.
WCF on page 58.

313. Mast, Gerald. *The Comic Mind: Comedy and the Movies.* Indianapolis: Bobbs-Merrill Co., 1973. 353pp.
WCF on pages x, 25, 34, 40, 42, 45, 145, 200, 204, 205, 218, 280, 281, 288, 293, 301, 320, 322.

314. Michael, Paul. *The American Movies Reference Book: The Sound Era.* New Jersey: Prentice-Hall, 1969. 629pp.
WCF on pages 21, 106, 309.

315. Moger, Art. *Some of My Best Friends Are People.* Boston: Little, Brown & Co., 1964. 156pp.
WCF on pages 39–40.

316. Montgomery, John. *Comedy Films: First Factual History of Men and Women Who Since 1894 Kept Us Laughing in the Cinema.* London: Allen & Unwin, 1954. 337pp.
WCF on pages 65, 244–245, 298.

317. Monti, Carlotta with Cy Rice. *W. C. Fields & Me.* New Jersey: Prentice-Hall, c1971. 227pp.
Carlotta Monti's memoirs.

318. Mordden, Ethan. *The Hollywood Musical.* New York: St. Martin's Press, c1981. 261pp.
WCF on pages 56, 75, 92, 157.

319. Morehouse, Ward. *Matinee Tomorrow: Fifty Years of Our Theatre.* New York: McGraw-Hill, 1949. 340pp.
WCF on pages 75, 133, 166, 208, 303.

320. Morino, Marianne. *The Hollywood Walk of Fame.* Berkeley: Ten Speed Press, c1987. 396pp.
WCF on pages 101, 356. Fields biographical data is inaccurate. Fields has two stars; one for radio, and one for films. Radio: 6316½ Hollywood Blvd. Films: 7004 Hollywood Blvd.

321. Murray, Ken. *The Body Merchant: The Story of Earl Carroll.* Pasadena: Ward Ritchie Press, c1976. 243pp.
WCF on pages [ix], 112, 135–138, 140–143, 146, 150, 192, 210. [Photos between pages 102–103.]

322. ________. *Life on a Pogo Stick: Autobiography of a Comedian.* New York: Holt, Rinehart & Winston, c1960. 180pp.
WCF on pages 79, 85. Photos facing pp. 116, 179.

323. Nash, Charles Edgar. *Trailer Ahoy!* Lancaster, Pennsylvania: Intelligencer Printing Co., 1937. 261pp.
WCF on pages [35–37].

324. National Vaudeville Artists. *May 3, 1925, Ninth Annual Benefit Keith-Albee N.Y. Hippodrama-Metropolitan Opera House, Manhattan Opera House, New Amsterdam Theatre, Knickerbocker Theatre.* New York: National Vaudeville Artists Benefit Fund, c1925. [558]pp.
Fields was #51 on a program of 197 performers.

325. Neibaur, James L. *Movie Comedians: The Complete Guide.* Jefferson, North Carolina: McFarland, 1986. 247pp.
WCF on pages 1, 2, 4, 57, 93, 100–108, 137, 164, 169, 241.

326. Oppenheimer, George. ed. *Passionate Playgoer.* New York: Viking Press, 1958. 623pp.
WCF on pages 138–140.

327. Parish, James R. and William T. Leonard, et al. *The Funsters.* New York: Arlington House, c1979. 752pp.
WCF on pages 104n, 114, 123, 145, 163, 166, 243, 244, 248, 262, 263–273, 307, 352.

328. ________. *Hollywood on Hollywood.* New Jersey: Scarecrow Press, 1978. 434pp.
WCF on pages 1, 32–34, 112, 265–266, 372, 399–401.

329. Parker, Brant and Johnny Hart. *Wizard of Id: Strike the Sot!* New York: Andrews and McMeel, c1988. 128pp.
WCF characterization: Larsen E. Pettyfogger on pages [7, 8, 13, 28, 43, 47, 62, 80, 97, 107, 111, 115, 128].

330. Pearson, Bill. *The W. C. Fields Book.* New York: Wonderful Publishing Co., c1973. 38pp.
Witzend 9. Issued with extra cover painting by Jeff Jones. Illustrated with the Shelby Kirch collection of stills. Contains the W. C. Fields game of Adversity, with official rules, and an interview of vaudevillian Allan Wood. Pearson created biographical data for each of Fields' pseudonyms.

331. Peary, Danny. ed. *Close-Ups: Intimate Profiles of Movie Stars by Their Co-Stars, Directors, Screenwriters and Friends.* New York: Workman Publishing, c1978. 606pp.
WCF on pages 18–22, 64, [97], 149, 151, 209, 576.

332. Rella, Ettore. *San Francisco Theatre Research Series: A Monograph History of the San Francisco Stage and Its People from 1849 to the Present Day.* Edited by Lawrence Estavan. Volume 14. San Francisco: Work Projects Administration, 1940. 343*l.*
Project 10677, O. P. 665-08-3-167. WCF on pages 305–306.

333. Rice, Alice Hegan. *Mrs. Wiggs of the Cabbage Patch.* New York: Grosset & Dunlap, [1934]. 154pp.

"A Paramount Photoplay." Front and rear end-papers have 16 photos from the film (W. C. Fields, ZaSu Pitts, Pauline Lord).

334. Robinson, David. *The Great Funnies: A History of Film Comedy.* New York: Studio Vista/Dutton Pictureback, c1969. 160pp.
WCF on pages 7, 62, 88, 96–97, 111, 125.

335. Sachs, Charles. *The Scriptorium. Catalogue No. Two.* Original letters, manuscripts & documents of famous people. Beverly Hills: Scriptorium, [1974]. [32]pp.
Page 12, photo's and description of Fields memorabilia.

336. Sarris, Andrew. *The American Cinema: Directors and Directions, 1929–1968.* New York: Dutton, 1968. 383pp.
WCF on pages 238–239.

337. Saunders, Allen and Elmer Woggon. *Big Chief Wahoo and the Great Gusto.* Based on the famous comic strip. Racine, Wisconsin: Whitman Pub. Co., c1938. pp. 424, [8].
Big Little Book #1443. Cover title: *Big Chief Wahoo.* The Great Gusto character is based on W. C. Fields.

338. ________. *Big Chief Wahoo and the Magic Lamp.* Based on the famous comic strip. Racine, Wisconsin: Whitman Pub. Co., c1940. pp. 424, [8].
Big Little Book #1483.

339. Scagnetti, Jack. *Movie Stars in Bath Tubs.* Middle Village, New York: Jonathan David Publishers, Inc., c1975. 160pp.
WCF on page 133.

340. Schickel, Richard and A. Hurlburt. *The Stars: The Personalities Who Made the Movies.* New York: Dial Press, 1962. 287pp.
WCF on pages 109–110.

341. Scott, Kathryn Leigh. *Lobby Cards: The Classic Comedies.* The Michael Hawks Collection. Volume II. Los Angeles: Pomegranate Press, c1988. 176pp.
WCF on pages 8, 95–96, 99–102, 105–106, 135–136, 145–146, 175. Photos of six Fields cards.

342. ________. *Lobby Cards: The Classic Films.* The Michael Hawks

Collection. [Volume I]. Los Angeles: Pomegranate Press, c1987. 176pp.
WCF on pages 32–33, 94–95, 158–159, 176. Photos of three Fields cards.

343. Seldes, Gilbert. *Movies for the Millions: An Account of Motion Pictures, Principally in America.* London: B. T. Batsford Ltd., [1937]. 120pp.
WCF on pages 41, 43, 44, 67, 96, 97. Photos facing pages 43 and 55. Also published as *The Movies Come from America.* New York: Charles Scribner's Sons, 1937. 120pp. [same pagination].

344. Sennett, Mack. *King of Comedy* by Mack Sennett as told to Cameron Shipp. New York: Doubleday & Co, 1954. 284pp.
WCF on pages 12, 90, 103, 125, 264–268.

345. Shales, Tom and Kevin Brownlow, et al. *The American Film Heritage: Impressions from the American Film Institute.* Edited by Kathleen Karr. Washington, D.C.: Acropolis Books. Ltd., 1972. 184pp.
WCF on pages 82, 168–171.

346. Shipman, David. *The Great Movie Stars. The Golden Years.* New York: Bonanza Books, c1970. 576pp.
WCF on pages 82, 100, 133, 194–198, 267, 284, 330, 560. Book has an index of title changes for films shown in Great Britain.

347. Skolsky, Sidney. *Times Square Tintypes. Being Typewriter Caricatures of Those Who Made Their Names Along the Not So Straight and Very Narrow Path of Broadway.* Illustrated by Gard. New York: Ives Washburn Publisher, 1930. 291pp.
WCF on pages 114–118, 182, 252.

348. Slide, Anthony. *The Vaudevillians: A Dictionary of Vaudeville Performers.* Westport, Connecticut: Arlington House, c1981. pp. 172, [1].
WCF on pages [vii, xiii, 10, 12, 24], 53–54, [127, 128, 168, 172].

349. Smart, James. *W. C. Fields in Philadelphia.* Philadelphia: The Shackamaxon Society, Inc., c1972. 18pp.

This was the first book to publish Fields' correct birth date after his death. Fields had no birth certificate simply because there was no legal requirement to register births in Pennsylvania until January 1, 1906.

350. Smith, Bill. *The Vaudevillians.* New York: MacMillian Publishing Co., c1976. 278pp.
WCF on pages 10, 14, 38 46, 48–49, 111–112, 201, 202, 203. [Photos on pages 148, 163.]

351. Smith, H. Allen. *The Life and Legend of Gene Fowler.* New York: William Morrow & Co., 1977. 319pp.
WCF on pages 16, 183, [207], 212, 220, 238, 244, 258–259, 265–268, 271, [288–289], 290, 292. Page 258, line 17, Fields is misspelled "Felds."

352. ________. *Lost in the Horse Latitudes.* Illustrated by Leo Hershfield. New York: Doubleday, Doran & Co., Inc., 1944. 224pp.
WCF on pages 8, 191–203.

353. Smith, Ronald L. *Comedy on Record: The Complete Critical Discography.* New York: Garland Publishing, Inc., 1988. 728pp.
Not indexed. WCF on pages [18, 59, 60, 61, 71, 72, 149, 214–220, 221, 246, 268, 301, 302, 315, 367, 383, 384, 406, 409, 443, 545, 624, 644, 673, 675, 724, 725].

354. Sobel, Bernard. *Broadway Heartbeat: Memoirs of a Press Agent.* New York: Hermitage House, 1953. 352pp.
WCF on pages 123, 140–142, 148, 252.

355. ________. *Burleycue: An Underground History of Burlesque Days.* New York: Farrar & Rinehart, Inc., c1931. 284pp.
WCF on pages 91, 116–119.

356. ________. *A Pictorial History of Burlesque.* New York: Putnam, 1956, 194pp.
WCF on pages 98, 161–164.

357. ________. *A Pictorial History of Vaudeville.* New York: Citadel Press, c1961. 224pp.
WCF on pages [18, 33, 81]. Not indexed.

358. Spitzer, Marian. *The Palace.* With introduction by Brooks Atkinson. New York: Atheneum, 1969. 267pp.

1913 program poster on end-papers. WCF on pages 23, 40, 63, 71, 85, 126, 167, 209–210, 252. Drawing of Fields between pages 108–109.

359. Stein, Charles W. *American Vaudeville As Seen by Its Contemporaries.* Edited with Commentary. New York: Alfred A. Knopf, 1984. pp. 392, [4].

WCF on pages 223, 230, 241, 246–252, 337, 369.

360. Stickel, Christophe. *Autographs. Catalogue* 7. Daly City, California: Compiler, 1990. 26pp.

Early Fields photos on front and back covers of catalogue; pages 8–9 describe five autographed photos and letters from the Otis Junkins collection.

361. Stuart, Ray. ed. *Immortals of the Screen.* [Los Angeles]: Sherbourne Press, 1965. 224pp.

WCF on pages 113–114.

362. Swallow, John W. *Midwife to an Octopus.* Encino, California: Garden House Press, 1964. 157pp. Limited to 100 copies.

WCF on page 54. Photo of Fields between pages 28–29. Swallow wrote that in 1934 he offered to replace Louella Parsons *Hollywood Hotel* program on CBS with a Fields program as an enticement to get Fields to consider radio as a new career.

363. Tanner, Louise. *All the Things We Were.* New York: Doubleday, 1968. 362pp.

WCF on pages 43–45.

364. Taylor, Robert Lewis. *W. C. Fields: His Follies and Fortunes.* New York: Doubleday & Co., 1949. pp. 340, [1].

The first full-length biography of Fields. A condensation of eight installments appeared in the *Saturday Evening Post,* May 21 to July 9, 1949, and a 19 page condensation appeared in *Reader's Digest* in December 1949.

365. [Tibbles, Percy T]. *The Magician's Handbook: A Complete Encyclopedia of the Magic Art for Professional and Amateur Entertainers.* By "Selbit." Including valuable contributions from those magicians who have made their names famous during the past and present centuries. London: Dawbarn & Ward, Ltd., 1901. 188pp.

Second edition, 1902. Green cloth covers printed in black ink. Frontispiece added. Ads on inside front and rear covers. Ornaments at end of each chapter changed from first edition. pp. 188, v. *Third Edition,* 1904. Green cloth covers printed in red ink. pp. 188, [2].

Three copies of the first edition are known to be in U. S. collections, and one copy of each the second and third editions are in the author's collection.

WCF on pages 122–127.

366. Tierney, Tom. *Thirty from the 30's.* New Jersey: Prentice-Hall, c1974. [pp. 6, 60*l*., 6]pp.

Cover title: *Paperdolls for Grownups; Thirty from the 30's; Costumes of the Great Stars.* Has Fields paper doll with six costumes. Fields on rear cover.

367. Treadwell, Bill. *Fifty Years of American Comedy.* New York: Exposition Press, 1951. 241pp.

WCF on pages 47–50, 57, 136, 207, 225.

368. Tynan, Kenneth. *Curtains: Reviews, Plays, Events and Players.* New York: Atheneum, 1961. 495pp.

WCF on pages 211, 288, 352–358.

369. Villegas, Lucio A. ed. *Album de Cinelandia Biografias y Retratos Auténticos.* Los Angeles: Mac Printing Co., 1928. 201pp.

Biography and photo on pages 54–55.

370. Wagenknecht, Edward and Anthony Slide. *The Films of D. W. Griffith.* New York: Crown Publishers, Inc., c1975. 276pp.

WCF on pages 211–219.

371. Wallace, Irving, et al. *The Intimate Sex Lives of Famous People.* New York: Delacorte Press, c1981. 618pp.

WCF on pages 15–16.

372. Waller, Charles. *Magical Nights at the Theatre: A Chronicle,* by Charles Waller. . . . Melbourne: Gerald Taylor Publications, 1980. 256pp.

First edition limited to 1,000 numbered, autographed copies. WCF on page 120. Photo of Fields between pages 124–125.

373. Wayburn, Ned. *The Art of Stage Dancing: The Story of a Beautiful and Profitable Profession. A Manual of Stage-Craft.* New York: Ned Wayburn Studios of Stage Dancing, Inc., c1925. 382pp.
Trade edition. Photo of Fields opposite page 206.

374. Weber, Joan. *Tillie's Punctured Romance: A Love Comedy of Circus Life.* Based on the motion picture story by Joan Weber. New York: Jacobsen-Hodgkinson-Corporation, c1928. pp. 127, [3].
Paramount series "Popular Plays & Screen Library." Copyright by Paramount-Famous-Lasky Corporation. Front and rear covers illustrated with W. C. Fields, Chester Conklin, Louise Fazenda. Movie photos are on pages 11, 23, 38, 50, 72, 90, 108, 121.
The Fields film is not an adaptation of Edgar Smith's stage play, or the Marie Dressler film of the same name. Edgar Smith did not receive credit, nor did Al Christie or Paramount ever claim in their publicity that their *Tillie* was a remake. The "press book" alludes to similarities, then states, "A most unusual comedy with a title that was a big hit of its day. . . ." Use of the title *Tillie's Punctured Romance* was an exploitation device to sell an entirely different story.

375. Wertheim, Arthur Frank. *Radio Comedy.* New York: Oxford University Press, 1979. 439pp.
WCF on pages 231, 266, 293, 357, 361–363, 370.

376. West, Mae. *The Autobiography of Mae West: Goodness Had Nothing to Do With It.* New Jersey: Prentice-Hall, Inc., 1959. 271pp.
WCF on pages 27, 199–206. Photos between pages 178–179.

377. West, Robert. *The Rape of Radio.* New York: Rodin Publishing Co., c1941. 546pp.
WCF on pages 246, 249. Not indexed.

378. West, Wallace. *Alice in Wonderland: A Novelized Version of the*

Motion Picture "Alice in Wonderland" A Paramount Picture based upon the story by Lewis Carroll. Used by permission of Paramount Productions, Inc. Racine, Wisconsin: Whitman Publishing Co., c1934. [116]pp.

Dust jacket, front cover, and end-papers illustrated with photos from the film. Has 38 photos within the text.

379. ________. *Alice in Wonderland.* The story of the motion picture "Alice in Wonderland," a Paramount picture based upon the story by Lewis Carroll. Featuring Charlotte Henry as "Alice." Adapted by Wallace West. . . . Racine, Wisconsin: Whitman Publishing Co., 1934. 160pp.

Big Little Book, #759. Illustrated covers, and 77 black and white photos from the film.

380. [Whiteman, Robert]. *America: An Illustrated Diary of Its Most Exciting Years.* [Valencia, California]: AFE Press, c1972. 141pp.

WCF on end-papers, and pages 23, 28, 136, 139–141. Includes "Can-You-Keep-A-Straight-Face Quiz?" by W. C. Fields from *Liberty,* November 29, 1941.

381. Wilk, Max. *The Wit and Wisdom of Hollywood: From the Squaw Man to the Hatchet Man*; assembled, recorded, footnoted and edited by Max Wilk. New York: Warner Paperback Library, 1973. 399pp.

WCF on pages 107–112.

382. Wolverton, Monte. *Manipulating Cigar Boxes with W. C. Fields.* n.p.: W. C. Fields Productions, Inc., c1980. [6]pp.

Sold with Juggle Bug, Inc. Cigar Boxes.

383. Yanni, Nicholas. *W. C. Fields: Pyramid Illustrated History of the Movies.* Edited by Ted Sennett. New York: Pyramid Publications, c1974. 157pp.

Has a short bibliography, filmography, and is indexed.

384. Zeltner, Irwin F. *What the Stars Told Me: Hollywood in Its Heyday.* New York: Exposition Press, c1971. 182pp.

WCF on pages 43–51, 88.

Note: Photoplay *editions in this bibliography are numbers 190 Andrews; 209, 210 Carroll; 230–234 Dickens; 268 Ford; 333 Rice; 374 Weber; 378, 379 West.*

There are twenty-eight titles relating exclusively to W. C. Fields: Numbers 223 Coursdon; 229 Deschner; 242 Everson; 246 Ronald J. Fields; 247–259 W. C. Fields; 260 W. C. Fields, Jr.; 262 Finke; 273 Gehring; 286 Hansen; 317 Monti; 330 Pearson; 349 Smart; 364 Taylor; 382 Wolverton; 383 Yanni.

Periodicals

385. Agee, James. "Comedy's Greatest Era. Mack Sennett's Maniacs and Four Master Clowns Made Action Both Louder and Funnier Than Words." *Life* 27-10 (5 Sept. 1949): 70–82, 85–86, 88.

Fields presented Sennett with a special Oscar for "his lasting contribution to the comedy technique of the screen." Photo of Fields, Frank Capra, and Mack Sennett at the 1938 Academy Awards.

386. Argus. "W. C. Fields in a Robin Hood Spirit. Comedian in a New Screen Role After Winning Back His Health." *Literary Digest* 121 (20 June 1936): 19.

387. "Artists Who Entertained at Our Jubilee Dinner. Eighteen Principals Who Contributed Their Talents and Added Zest and Eclat to *Theatre* Magazine's Anniversary Celebration." *Theatre* 42 (July 1925): 30.

388. Aubyn, Maurice. "Dans la Peau du Lion." *Le Film Complet du Dimanche* 8-757 (8 Dec. 1929): 16pp.

Story adaptation, and 16 photos from *Running Wild.*

389. ________. "David Copperfield avec Freddie Bartholomew." *Le Film Complet du Samedi* 15-1793 (9 May 1936): 16pp.

Story adaptation with 18 photos from the film.

390. ________. "Le Don Juan du Cirque." *Le Film Complet du Mardi* 8-738 (5 Nov. 1929): 16pp.

Story adaptation with 12 photos from *Two Flaming Youths.*

391. Barbour, Alan. "W. C. Fields and Mae West." *Alan Barbour's Screen Nostalgia Illustrated* 1-1 (Nov. 1974): 40.

392. Barry, Barbara. "What to Expect in the New Films." *New Movie* 11 (Jan. 1935): 38–39, 71–72.
Review and photos from *It's a Gift.*

393. Barry, John K. "Ernst Lubitsch and the Comedy of the Thirties." *Mise-en-Scène* 1 [1970]: 7–10.

394. Baskette, Kirtley. "Humpty Dumpty Sat On a Wall, All the King's Men Couldn't Put Him Together Until the Amazing Truth About W. C. Fields' Return to Life." *Radio Mirror* 8-5 (Sept. 1937): 26–27, 73–74.

395. Beaudine, William. "Just a Lovable Old So and So." *Film Weekly* (7 Dec. 1934): 3, 37, 53.

396. Bellamy, Francis R. "W. C. Fields Series of Playlets In the Vanities." *Outlook* 149 (22 Aug. 1928): 670.

397. Beranger, Clara. "The Most Melancholy Funny Man on the Screen. The Strange Story of a Lonely, Forlorn, Embattled Figure Who Has Made Millions Laugh—A Close Up of a Comic, W. C. Fields." *Liberty* 13 (15 Feb. 1936): 31–32.
Fields is on the cover.

398. "Big Broadcast 1938." *Ciné-Miroir* 679 (8 Avril 1938): 219–220.
Photos with dialogue from the script.

399. Blackbeard, Bill. "Q's & A's about comic strips! The San Francisco Academy of Comic Art answers your questions on comic strips." *Cartoonist Profiles* 40 (Dec. 1978): 66–72.
Documents Fields' comic strip appearances.

400. Bloch, Robert. "The Unexplored Fields: Some New Lore to Set Aright the Old and Often Distorted Legends About the Greatest Wit of All, W. C. Fields." *Gent* 6-3 (Feb. 1962): 8–10, 51–52.

401. Borton, Elizabeth. "I Take a Juggling Lesson from W. C. Fields." *Hollywood* 24 (Sept. 1935): 37, 50–51.

402. Bradbury, Ray. "On Roller Skates in Hollywood." *Reader's Digest* 129 (Sept. 1986): 54–58.

403. "Brickbats and Bouquets." *Photoplay* 46 (Aug. 1934): 14.
Photo of Fields as "The Great McGonigle."

404. Brooks, Louise. "The Other Face of W. C. Fields." *Sight and Sound* 40 (Spring 1971): 92–96.

405. Broun, Heywood. "In the Star-Spangled Manner Florenz Ziegfeld Jr. Offers the 13th Annual Production of the Ziegfeld Follies Beginning Monday Evening June 24, 1918 as If by Heywood Broun." *Stage* 14 (Aug. 1937): 1, 64–66.
Article about the 1918 Follies with cast photo.

406. ———. "W. C. Fields and the Cosmos." *Nation* 132 (7 Jan. 1931): 24–25.

407. "The Camera Speaks at a Zanuck Party." *Photoplay* 53 (Dec. 1939): 33.
Photo of Fields with Fannie Brice.

408. [Cantwell, Robert E]. "With Wit and Love." *Newsweek* 43 (5 April 1954): 96–97.

409. Carle, Teet. "Beating the Drums for Another Comic of the Silents, W. C. Fields." *Los Angeles Times Calendar* (19 Dec. 1971): p. 22.

410. ———. "The Man Was Fascinated by Names." *Hollywood Studio Magazine* 6 (Feb. 1972): 11–13.

411. Carnegie, Dale. "Funny-man Fields. A Five-Minute Biography. . . ." *Scholastic* 31 (9 Oct. 1937): 7–9.

412. Cary, Harold. "The Loneliest Man in the Movies. W. C. Fields Didn't Achieve a Place in the Silent Drama Until He Found a Speaking Part." *Collier's* 76 (28 Nov. 1925): 26.

413. Cerf, Bennett. "Trade Winds." *Saturday Review of Literature* 27 (3 June 1944): 20.

414. ———. "Two Gents of the Old School: That Rollicking Pair, Barrymore and Fields, Are Gone, but Their Escapades Are Still Turning Up." *This Week* (14 Dec. 1958): 4–7.

415. "Charlie McCarthy and W. C. (sideline) Fields." *Stage* 16 (Feb. 1939): 32.
Photos from *You Can't Cheat an Honest Man.*

416. "Charlie McCarthy Is the Most Objectionable Young Man in America." *Life* 3 (26 July 1937): 57–58.

417. Cheatham, Maude. "Juggler of Laughs. W. C. Fields Can Balance a Plug Hat on a Cane or an Audience on a Gale of Laughter." *Silver Screen* 5 (April 1935): 30–31, 62.

418. Cherin, Barry. "W. C. Fields and Me. Valerie Meets the Real Carlotta." *Hollywood Studio Magazine* 10 (Sept. 1975): 7–9.

419. "Clang, Clang, Clang!" *Screen Book* 19 (Sept. 1937): 24–25.

420. "Clipped From the Interviews." *Film Fun* 64 (Sept. 1935): 17.
Photo from *Man on the Flying Trapeze.*

421. "Collector Item." *Movie Stars Parade* 4-6 (May 1944): 46.
Article and photos from *Follow the Boys.*

422. [Cole, Walter]. "At the Ziegfeld Follies. Various Entertainers in the Big Show as Seen by Theatre Magazine's Artist." *Theatre* 34 (Oct. 1921): 211.
Pen sketch of Fields as a parson.

423. Collins, Charles. "Good-by Mr. Quips!" *Chicago Sunday Tribune* (9 Feb. 1947): 7, 20.

424. "The Comic—W. C. Fields." *Vanity Fair* 42 (June 1934): 32.

425. "Commuting with an Automobile Trailer." *Everyday Science and Mechanics* (Oct. 1934): 538.

426. "Complaint Dept." (W. C. Fields wants to cancel $50,000.00 annuity.) *Time* 38 (20 Oct. 1941): 68.

427. Condon, Frank. "Little Known Facts About Well-Known Golfers." *Saturday Evening Post* 204 (5 March 1932): 33–35.

428. Conlon, Scoop. "W. C. Fields Speaks His Mind: Startling Expose! W. C. Tells What He Thinks of All Directors, Especially Gregory La Cava." *Screen Play* 19 (Feb. 1936): 50, 81.

429. Cooper, Arthur. "His Last Chickadee." *Newsweek* 77 (21 June 1971): 92–93.

430. Crowther, Bosley. "W. C. Fields: His Follies & Fortunes," by Robert Lewis Taylor. *Book Find News* 84 (1949): 2–5.
Review and 19 photos.

431. Darnton, Charles. "Barrymore Makes a True Confession." *Hollywood* 26 (Feb. 1938): 28–29, 64–65.

Six photos of Fields and Barrymore; they were scheduled to appear together in Paramount's *Things Begin to Happen.*

432. ________. "Mr. Fields Wins by a Nose: The Sprightly Comedian Found Dying Too, Too Funny. Now He's Settled Down to the Serious Job of Living—and New Fame and Fortune Have Crowned His Efforts and Rewarded His Virtue." *Screen Book* 19 (Nov. 1937): 34–35, 105.
Screen Book for November combined with *Screen Play.*

433. "David Copperfield. This Is the Way Dickens' Classic Looks on the Screen." *Photoplay* 47 (March 1935): 52–53.

434. Dessaignes, R. "International House avec Peggy Hopkins Joyce et Sari Maritza." *Le Film Complet du Jeudi* 13-1504 (5 July 1934): 16pp.
Story adaptation with 13 photos from the film.

435. "Dickens' David Copperfield." (Photos.) *Motion Picture* 47 (Feb. 1935): 22–23.

436. Dowling, Mark. "Test Your Sense of Humor!" *Silver Screen* 6-28 (Oct. 1936): 64–65.

437. Durgnat, Raymond. "Subversion in the Fields." *Films and Filming* 12 (Dec. 1965): 42–48.

438. Early, Dudley. "The Gentleman Speaks His Mind: Why Did I Quit Radio? Am I Mad at Charlie McCarthy and Bergen? What Do I Think of Censors? Why Don't I Buy a Yacht? Was I Ever Drunk? What's Wrong with My Nose? W. C. Fields 'Tells All.'" *Family Circle* 12 (8 April 1938): 10–11, 22.
Fields on front cover.

439. "Eccentric's Eccentric." *Time* 63 (5 April 1954): 108.

440. Engel, Lyle K. ed. "The Big Broadcast of 1938." *Song Hits* 1–6 (Feb. 1938): 10–11.
Roster of cast with 18 photos from the film.

441. ________. "The Big Broadcast." *Song Lyrics* 1-3 (March 1938): 12–13.
Two pages of photos from the film.

442. ________. "Chase and Sanborn Hour." *Song Hits* 2-12 (May 1939): 22.

Article with photo of Fields, Bergen, and McCarthy.

443. Evans, Carol. "The Sounds of Silence: Comedy of the Twenties." *Mise-en-Scène* 1 [1970]: 23–27.

444. Evans, Harry. "Hollywood Diary. Why Did Those Who Movies Predict That the Mae West–W. C. Fields Combination Would Be Dynamite? The Author Gets a Slant on It by Visiting Bill and Mae on the Lot." *Family Circle* 16-12 (22 March 1940): 14–15, 16, 18–19, 23.
Fields on cover; four photos in article.

445. "Famous Characters Come Alive in 16mm." *Film and Radio Guide* 12 (April 1946): 42.
Same photo as December, 1945 issue.

446. "Famous Comedian Demonstrates the Restrained Way to Eat Mince Pie!" *Photoplay* 47 (Dec. 1934): 3.
Ad for None-Such Mince Meat.

447. "Favorite Punch Recipies." *Film Fun* 62 (Nov. 1934): 33.
Photo from *The Old Fashioned Way.*

448. Fender, Bob. "Nuts to You!" *Hollywood* 22 (Dec. 1933): 24, 62.

449. Ferguson, Otis C. "The Great McGonigle." *New Republic* 84 (21 Aug. 1935): 48.

450. ________. "Happy Endings." *New Republic* 105 (10 Nov. 1941): 622.

451. ________. "Movies, Light and Heavy." *New Republic* 79 (1 Aug. 1934): 320.

452. ________. "The Old Fashioned Way." *New Republic* 103 (30 Dec. 1940): 900.

453. "Field Day." *Movie Life* 7 (July 1944): 56–57.
Six photos from *Song of the Open Road,* and *Sensations of 1945.*

454. "Fields Day!" (Photos.) *Film Fun* 61 (Jan. 1934): 28–29, 48.

455. Fields, Ronald J. "The Adventures and Mis-Adventures of W. C. Fields." *Argosy* 380 (Aug. 1974): 68–69, 71.

456. Fields, W. C. "Alcohol and Me." *Pic* 9 (13 Oct. 1942): 32–34.

457. ________. "Anything for a Laugh." *American Magazine* 118 (Sept. 1934): 129–130.

458. ________. "Can-You-Keep-a-Straight-Face Quiz?" *Liberty* 18 (29 Nov. 1941): 30, 40.

459. ________. "The Care of Babies." *This Week* (18 Feb. 1940): 12, 22.

460. ________. "Danger . . . The Great Man Is At Work." *Look* 4-25 (3 Dec. 1940): 54–55.
Photo of Fields with his secretary Malinda Boss.

461. ________. "From Boy Juggler to Star Comedian. One Fun-Maker's Income, Beginning with Five Dollars a Week, Now Exceeds Five Thousand for the Same Period." *Theatre* 48 (Oct. 1928): 44, 76.

462. ________. "The Good Old Days of Vaudeville." *Coronet* 15 (Dec. 1943): 99–113.
Picture story with 34 photos.

463. ________. "How to Figure Your Income Tax." *This Week* (10 March 1940): 7, 16.

464. ________. "How to Make New Year's Resolutions." *This Week* (31 Dec. 1941): 6, 10.

465. ________. "I Have Found the New Preparation Orchidew Excellent for Use after Shaving." *Theatre* 41 (Feb. 1925): 51.
Ad for Orchidew Cleansing Skin Lotion.

466. ________. "Life Begins at Twenty Says W. C. Fields." *Motion Picture* 50 (Sept. 1935): 49, 70–71.

467. ________. "Life Begins at Twenty." *Picturegoer Weekly* 5 (26 Oct. 1935): 16–17.

468. ________. "My Rules of Etiquette." *This Week* (4 Dec. 1938): 6, 15.

469. ________. "My Views on Marriage." *This Week* (15 Oct. 1939): 7, 19.

470. ________. "Reply to Mr. Freed." *Goad* 2 (1951): 29.

471. ________. "This Radio Gadget." *Radio Guide* 7-3 (6 Nov. 1937): 6.

472. "Fifty Filmographies." *Film Comment* 6 (Winter 1970–71): 101–116.

473. Flatley, Guy. "A Fields-Eye View of Things." *New York Times Magazine* (24 April 1966): 117.

474. ________. "Who Was He?" *New York Times Magazine* (24 April 1966): 114.

475. Flinn, Tom. "Out of the Past. Harold Lloyd and W. C. Fields." *Velvet Light Trap* 3 (Winter 1971-72): 6–7.

476. "Follow the Boys." (Photos.) *Song Parade* 3 (Aug. 1944): 4–5.

477. Fontron, Elizabeth. "W. C. Fields Hated to Get Up in the Morning and So. . . ." *Cinema Art* 6 (Aug. 1927): 44, 47.

478. Ford, Corey. "Eustace McGargle, Egbert Sousé, Otis Criblecoblis, Cuthbert J. Twillie, Figley J. Whitesides, Dr. Otis Guelpe, Larson E. Whipsnade, Chester Bogle, or, the one and only W. C. Fields." *Harpers* 235 (Oct. 1967): 65–68.

479. ________. "Offstage Glimpses of an Outrageous Comic Genius: W. C. Fields, the One and Only, Condensed from *The Time of Laughter.*" *Reader's Digest* 91 (Nov. 1967): 158–162.

480. Fowler, Gene. "My Old Friends." *Diners' Club Magazine* (Oct. 1960): 33, 50–52.

481. Fowler, Will. "A Holiday Visit with W. C. Fields: Sleigh Bells Give Me Double Nausea!" *Life* 73 (15 Dec. 1972): 42.

482. ________. "Why W. C. Fields Hated Christmas: A Holiday Fable." *Show Business Illustrated* 1 (2 Jan. 1962): 115–116.

483. Frank, Nino. "Les Films Nouveaux: The Big Broadcast of 1938." *Pour Vous* (6 Avril 1938): 28.

484. Freeman, C. Mitchell. ed. "W. C. Fields Tips to Picnickers." *1000 Jokes* 126 (June-Aug. 1968): 24–25.
Fields on cover.

485. "Funnyman W. C. Fields Has His Own Way of Keeping Himself Fit." *Life* 10 (12 May 1941): 104–106, 109.

486. Gabriel, Gilbert W. "Good Looks to Great Laughter. Hollywood Can Have Its Glamour, but Great Comedians Belong to the Stage." *Stage* 13 (Feb. 1938): 38–41.

487. Gammie, John. "Copperfield Comes to Life!" *Film Weekly* 14-361 (13 Sept. 1935): 2, 34.

488. "Gaumont Company Releases During the Week of Sept. 19th W. C. Fields in *Pool Sharks*. Casino Star Comedy." *Motion Picture News* 12 (2 Oct. 1915): 103.

489. "Gaumont Pictures on Mutual Program All Made Here!" *Motion Picture News* 12 (30 Oct. 1915): 80.

490. "Gaumont Stars." *Motion Picture News* 12 (23 Oct. 1915): 111.

491. "Gentle Grifter." *Time* 40 (6 Jan. 1947): 54.

492. "Ghosts of W. C. Fields: Whom Did He Marry?" *Newsweek* 38 (10 Sept. 1951): 28–29.

493. Gillespie-Hayek, Annabelle. "Oh What a Dummy! The Torment of Bill Fields and Don Ameche." *Silver Screen* 7 (Oct. 1937): 18–19.

494. Gilliatt, Penelope. "The Current Cinema: To W. C. Fields Dyspeptic Mumbler, Who Invented His Own Way Out." *New Yorker* 45 (21 June 1969): 86, 89–90.

495. Gilson, Paul. "Vive le Mélodrame: où Margot ne pleure plus." *Pour Vous* 343 (13 Juin 1935): 20–21.
Article and photos from *The Old Fashioned Way*.

496. Glover, Edwin W. "Pictures with a Past: Remember When?" *Saturday Evening Post* 228 (15 Oct. 1955): 17.

497. Grady, Lester C. "For Distinguished Service to Radio." *Radio Stars* 1 (Aug. 1937): 19.

498. Grant, Jack. "Proud of His Big Nose." *Movie Classic* 7 (Feb. 1935): 56, 60.

499. "Great Impersonations: Mr. W. C. Fields as Queen Victoria." *Stage* 1 (Dec. 1940): 43.

500. Hall, Gladys. "Have You Got the Makings of a Comedian? Six Famous Funsters Tell You What It Takes to Be a Comic." *Movie Classic* 7 (Dec. 1934): 30–31, 68.

501. Hall, Warren. "Secret Sentiment of W. C. Fields." *American Weekly* (9 March 1947): 13.

502. Hamilton, Sara. "Dangerous Days for Bill Fields. Illness Casts Its Sinister Shadow Over Hollywood's Most Beloved Comedian, but He Carries Merrily On." *Photoplay* 50 (July 1936): 30–31, 108–109.

503. ________. "A Red Nose Romeo. Let W. C. Goose-Step Out—and Hollywood's Handsome Heroes Don't Get a Tumble." *Photoplay* 47 (Dec. 1934): 32–33.

504. ________. "That Man's Here Again." *Photoplay* 51 (Aug. 1937): 16, 103–104.

505. Handlin, Oscar. "Fear and Laughter." *Atlantic* 221 (Jan. 1968): 116, 118.

506. Hanemann, Helen. "He Hated Alarm-Clocks and Proves That Old Saying About the Early Worm Is Not to Be Taken Too Seriously." *Motion Picture* 32 (Aug. 1926): 39, 98.

507. Hermer, Cal. ed. "Increased Manpower; Paramount Pictures, 1936–37." *Box Office* 29-4 (20 June 1936).

Fields on cover. Central edition.

508. ________. ed. "Forty Paramount Releases During First Half Season." *Box Office* 29-3 (13 June 1936): 11.

Fields on cover. Central edition.

509. "High Hat." (Photo of Fields.) *Motion Picture Classic* 23 (April 1926): 62.

510. "Hollywood: A Page of Gossip from the West Coast." *Theatre* 46 (Nov. 1927): 45, 56.

511. Holmes, John Clellon. "Uncle Willy and Us." *Audience* 1 (Jan. 1971): 4–9.

512. [Hornblow, Arthur]. "Mr. Hornblow Goes to the Play." (Poppy.) *Theatre* 38 (Nov. 1923): 19, 29.

513. Howe, Herb. "Hollywood, Past and Future." *New Movie* 11 (Jan. 1935): 44–45, 54.

Howe rates Fields among the 13 best actors in Hollywood, and as the best comedian.

514. "How Funny Mr. Fields Cashes in on His Jinx: Persistent Misfortunes, Both Serious and Trivial, Which the Popular

Comedian Turns into Gags and Wise-Cracks and Lots of Money." *American Weekly* (17 Oct. 1937): 7.

515. "How the Films Fought Shy of Bill Fields." *Literary Digest* 88 (20 Feb. 1926): 52–54.

516. Hynd, Alan. "Esquiregraph No. 9—W. C. Fields." *Esquire* 24-1 (July 1945): 168–169.

517. "If You Were Born in 1934." *Newsweek* 64 (17 Aug. 1964): 35.
New England Life ad; photo from *Tillie & Gus.*

518. "In Philly No Cigar for W. C. Fields." *Us Magazine* 4 (5 Feb. 1980): 4.

519. "Index, Directors, Players, Producers." *The Movies 1940 and the People Who Make Them* 2 (March 1940): 14–15.

520. "It Wasn't So Long Ago." (Photos from Mississippi.) *Film Fun* 64 (July 1935): 32.

521. "It's the Old Army Game—This Soda Business." (Photos.) *Motion Picture Classic* 23 (July 1926): 44.

522. Jackson, Michael. "We Cover the Studios." *Photoplay* 49 (June 1936): 46–47.

523. Jacobs, Jay. "Days of Wine and Legends." *Reporter* 38 (25 Jan. 1968): 49–50.

524. Jaderquist, Eugene. "Gene Fowler: Hollywood's Most Fabled Writer." *Modern Man* 6 (Nov. 1956): 12–14, 49.

525. Janis, Elsie. "I Was That Way About W. C. Fields." *New Movie* 11 (Jan. 1935): 24–25, 58.

526. "January 29th Tribute to W. C. Fields. . . ." *Films in Review* 31 (May 1980): 315.

527. Johnston, Alva. "Local Man." *New Yorker* 22 (25 Jan. 1947): 18–19.

528. ———. "Legitimate Nonchalance." *New Yorker* 10 (2 Feb.): 23–26; (9 Feb.): 25–28; (16 Feb. 1935): 22–26.
Biography of Fields.

529. ———. "Who Knows What Is Funny?" *Saturday Evening Post* 211 (6 Aug. 1938): 10–11, 43, 45–46.

530. Kaplan, Peter W. "W. C. Fields at 100." *Film Comment* 15 (March-April 1979): 57–59.

531. Kendall, Robert. "Collecting W. C. Fields & Mae West Memorabilia." *Hollywood Studio Magazine* 15-6 (March 1982): 32.

532. Kindler, Jan. "Elysian Fields: No Man Who Hated Dogs, Children, Virgins, Teetotalers, Churchgoers, Henpeckers, Brownnoses, Eggheads, Bluestockings, Twaddlers and Nincompoops the Way W. C. Did Could Have Been All Bad." *Playboy* 16 (March 1969): 116–118, 187–188, 190–192, 194, 196–199.

533. "Kings of Comedy Who Have Long Reigned on Broadway by Successfully Humoring Their Subjects." *Theatre* 44 (Oct. 1926): 19.

534. Kingsley, Myra. "Shadows in the Stars." *Radio Mirror* 9 (Feb. 1938): 18, 54–56.
Fields' horoscope.

535. Kresh, Paul. "W. C. Fields' Continuing Legacy." *Stereo Review* 34 (April 1975): 90.

536. "Laughter." *Screen Album* (Fall 1936): 39.

537. Lee, Raymond. "The Brabbling Boozer Returns." *Classic Film Collector* 24 (Summer 1969): 46–47.

538. "Letters to the Editor." *Life* 6 (6 Feb. 1939): 4.
Comparison of Lucius Beebe photo to that of Fields two decades earlier.

539. "Letters to the Editor: *Movie Classic* Invites Its Readers to Air Their Opinion of Pictures and Stars and Offers Prizes for the Best Letters." *Movie Classic* 8 (May 1935): 10, 70.
Letter from reader with photo of Fields as Micawber.

540. Little, Barbara. "Laziness Made Him What He Is To-day." *Picture Play* 23 (Oct. 1925): 25, 94.

541. "Looking Back with Us." *Us Magazine* 4 (27 May 1980): 78.

542. "Looking Foward. W. C. Fields to Star in So's Your Old Man: Following This Production He Will Appear in The Wild Man Man of Borneo." *Paris and Hollywood* 2 (June 1926): 96.

543. McCarten, John. "The Current Cinema: Ring in the Old." *New Yorker* 25 (25 June 1949): 77–78.

544. MacArthur, Mildred. "Watch Out for My Putter, Chickadee, or I'll Bury Your Head in a Sandtrap." *Los Angeles* 20 (April 1975): 55.

Author is the wife of Arthur McArthur of Beyer & MacArthur; Fields' last agent was Charles Beyer.

545. McCarthy, Charlie. "The Man I Hate and Vice Versa, as Told to Dorothy Spensley." *Radio Mirror* 9 (Dec. 1937): 18–19, 67–70.

Fields/McCarthy on cover.

546. McEvoy, J. P. "He Knew What They Wanted." *Saturday Evening Post* 205 (10 Sept. 1932): 10–11, 51–52.

547. ________. "W. C. Fields' Best Friend. We'll Give You One Guess. It's W. C. Fields. In 50 Years of Comedy He's Always Had the Last Laugh." *This Week* (26 July 1942): 15–16.

548. McGee, John. "Reel Reviewer. Sally of the Sawdust." *Classic Images Review* 62 (March 1979): 45.

549. McVay, Douglas. "Elysian Fields." *Film* 50 (Winter 1967-68): 22–23.

550. "Mae and Bill Out West." *Newsweek* 16 (26 Feb. 1940): 30.

551. "Mae Still Gets 'Em! Three Men Come Up to See a New West in My Little Chickadee!" *Screen Guide* 4 (March 1940): 39, 46, 48.

552. "Man on the Flying Trapeze." *Film Weekly* 14-353 (19 July 1935): 19.

553. "Man's Best Friend." (Photo.) *Newsweek* 26 (5 Nov. 1945): 81.

554. Markfield, Wallace. "The Dark Geography of W. C. Fields." *New York Times Magazine* (24 April 1966): 32–33, 110, 112, 116, 119, 120.

555. Marlowe, Don. "Fieldsiana: From the Hollywood That Was by Don Marlowe." *Classic Film Collector* 28 (Fall 1970): 48.

Formerly *8mm Collector*. Current title: *Classic Images Review*.

556. Mason, Arthur. "Radio Ramblings." *Radio Stars* 11 (Aug. 1937): 6–7.

557. ________. "Radio Ramblings." *Radio Stars* 11 (Oct. 1937): 6–7, 68–69, 92–94.
Fields on cover.

558. Matthews, Francis Barr. "Hollywood's Most Dramatic Story. Funnyman W. C. Fields Has Been Playing the Pagliacci Role Long Enough. It's Time You Learned the Truth About His Heroism." *Screen Guide* 1 (July 1936): 16–17, 43.

559. "Mental Gaps: Psychologist Ascertains How Human Mind Snatches Rest-Periods." *Literary Digest* 122 (29 Aug. 1936): 19.
Discusses Fields' mind-block word habits.

560. "M-G-M's Notable Screen Version of *David Copperfield.* Now at Last Available in 16mm for Classroom Use." *Film and Radio Guide* 12-3 (Dec. 1945): 60.

561. Miller, Don. "Films on T.V." *Films in Review* 13 (Aug.-Sept. 1962): 433–434.

562. Miller, Llewellyn. "Casanova Comes to Town." *Screen Play* 21 (Aug. 1937): 22–23, 81.

563. Miroël, Yves. "Ce Bon Mr. Hunter." *Le Film Complet du Jeudi* 9-815 (20 March 1930): 16pp.
Story adaptation and 12 photos from *Fools for Luck.*

564. Miron, Charles. "The Sweet-and-Sour Success Story of W. C. Fields." *Motion Picture* 58 (Feb. 1970): 60–65, 92.
Series title: Nostalgia: The 6th in a series of Hollywood immortals.

565. "More Power to You!" *Film Fun* 64 (Oct. 1935): 18, 38.
Photos from *Man on the Flying Trapeze.*

566. Morgan, Don. "Godfrey Daniels! W. C. Dukenfield Has Returned." *Los Angeles Times Calendar* (21 Jan. 1968): 12.

567. Morgan, Harry H. "W. C. Fields' Embattled Fortune." *American Weekly* (16 Oct. 1949): 11.

568. Morehouse, Ward. "Postscript to '23." *Theatre Arts* 32 (Fall 1948): 44.

569. "Movie Life of W. C. Fields." *Movie Life* 2-3 (March 1939): 36–39.
Fields, Bergen, and McCarthy on cover.

570. "Movies: Screen Openings, *The Bank Dick.*" *Newsweek* 16 (16 Dec. 1940): 67–68.

571. Mullett, Mary B. "Bill Fields Disliked His Label, So He Laughed It Off. He Wanted to Be a Comedian, but the Theatrical World Had Him Tagged as a Comedy Juggler, and It Took Him Ten Years to Get Rid of That Tag. He Tells Here the Remarkable Story of His Career, Which Began When, at the Age of Eleven, He Ran Away from Home." *American Magazine* 101 (Jan. 1926): 18–19, 143–147.

572. Murray, Feg. "Seein' Stars." *Classic Images* 155 (May 1988): 4.
Reprint of No. 155. King Features Syndicate, Inc., copyright 1936. Drawing of Fields as Micawber.

573. "Mutual Program. Rialto Theatre Stars." (Photos.) *Moving Picture World* 25 (18 Sept. 1915): 2037.

574. "My Little Chickadee. Mae West and W. C. Fields Burlesque the Westerns." *Life* 8 (19 Feb. 1940): 63–65.

575. "My Little Chickadee." *The Movies 1940 and the People Who Make Them* (Feb. 1940): 224.
[Film review service.]

576. "My Little Chickadee with Mae West and W. C. Fields." *Look* 4-6 (12 March 1940): 42–45.

577. "Never Give a Sucker an Even Break Starring W. C. Fields." *Movie Story* 17 (Dec. 1941): 53–54, 56, 58.

578. Newton, Jim. "On the Air." *Photoplay* 51 (Sept. 1937): 64–65, 92, 94.

579. North, Christopher. "MGM's First 30 Years." (Photo with caption "Fields Micawbered Bartholomew.") *Films in Review* 5 (May 1954): 219.

580. "Nosy Fields, a Teetotaler, by Gad." *Literary Digest* (26 June 1937): 9.

581. "Passport Photos You May Have Missed. A Gallery of Miscellaneous Rogues, Caught by the Camera at the Point of Departure." *Vanity Fair* 28 (July 1927): 47.

582. "People." (Photo.) *Time* 34 (25 Sept. 1939): 53.
Back in court with Dr. Jesse Citron.

583. "People." (Photo.) *Time* 30 (4 Oct. 1937): 68.
Fight with Carlotta Monti.

584. "People." (Fields postage stamp.) *Time* 115 (11 Feb. 1980): 66.
Government paid Fields' heirs $2,023.00 royalty to print a postage stamp in his honor.

585. Perine, Fred J. ed. "W. C. Fields Who Furnishes the Comedy in 'Sally of the Sawdust' at the Strand This Week." *Screenland* 5-25 (31 Oct. 1925): 1, 5.

586. Plummer, Evans. "Along the Airialtos: Hollywood." *Movie Radio Guide* 10 (11-17 Jan. 1941): 38–39.
Three photos of Fields at a party for Rudy Vallee.

587. "Pompous Bluff, the Genial Fraud." *Nation* 164 (4 Jan. 1947): 3.

588. "Poppy." (Photo.) *Stage* 13 (June 1936): 11, 41.
Fields on cover.

589. Prelutsky, Burt. "Deja Nose. W. C. Fields Is Alive and Well in Bill Oberlin." *Los Angeles Times West* (7 Feb. 1971): 5.

590. ________. "Woody and the Chinaman. Carlotta Monti Gave Up a Promising Movie Career to Devote 14 Years to Pampering W. C. Fields." *Los Angeles Times West* (26 May 1968): 8–12.
Cover: "W. C. Fields wasn't all bad." Photo.

591. "Presenting W. C. Fields. The Indefatigable Comedian May Be Discovered in His Element in the New Vanities." *Vanity Fair* 31 (Nov. 1928): 63.

592. "Pre-showing of 'Tillie's Punctured Romance.'" (Photos and credits.) *Screenland* 16 (April [*sic*] 1928): 59, 80.
Cover date should read [March].

593. Priestly, J. B. "W. C. Fields." *New Statesman* 33 (4 Jan. 1947): 8.

594. ________. "W. C. Fields." *Atlantic* 179 (March 1947): 43–44.

595. Prior, Moody E. "In Search of the Grampian Hills with W. C. Fields." *American Scholar* 48 (Winter 1978-79): 101–105.

596. "Private Lives." (Photo.) *Life* 2 (28 June 1937): 84.
Fields is sued for $12,000.00.

597. "Readers Row." (Photo as Micawber.) *Motion Picture* 49 (May 1935): 12.

598. "Recordings." *Playboy* 22 (April 1975): 26.

599. Redway, Sara. "W. C. Fields: Pleads for Rough Humor." *Motion Picture Classic* 22 (Sept. 1925): 32–33, 73.

600. Regan, Jack and Grace Reed. "The Two Sides of W. C. Fields: There's the Cuckoo Side Which Makes You Feel That He's Stepped out of One of His Movies. — Then There's the Unexpected Side that Shows You the Half-Naked Homeless Lad Who Became the Man You Learn to Know in These Two Fine Stories." *Movie Mirror* 6 (April 1935): 38–39, 69–72.

601. Reid, J. "Nobody's Dummy. Bill Fields, Little Chickadees, Is No Termites Flophouse, Sitting on a Ventriloquist's Knee. He's a Born Comic Who Stands on His Own Hind Legs, Passing Wisecracks and Quick on the Pickup." *Motion Picture* 54 (Oct. 1937): 37, 84–86.

602. Rense, Rip and Charles Bogle. "W. C. Fields Was 'Uncle Claude' to Him." *Valley News* (19 Jan. 1979): 1–2, 14, 17, 21.
Article by Will Fowler.

603. Rich, Gene. ed. "Who Says There No Santa Claus?" *Box Office* 31-26 (20 Nov. 1937): 1.
Central edition. Photo of Fields as Santa.

604. "Right Paper in the Customers Pocket." *Educational Dealer* 7-32 (March 1982): 32.
Georgia Pacific ad. Full page drawing of Fields.

605. Riley, Thomas Nord. "Battle of the Sexes." *Hollywood* 29 (March 1940): 23, 52–53.

606. ________. "Bottle Baby." *Motion Picture* 58 (May 1944): 102–103.

607. Robert, Claudio L. "A todo gas. Adaptación en forma de la película del mismo título, interpretada por el gracioso actor americano Jack Okie (W. C. Fields, Susan Fleming)." *Selección Films de Amor* 11-586 (n.d.): 2-32.

Six photos from *Million Dollar Legs.* Paramount, 1932. Published in Barcelona. "Aparece los Martes."

608. Roberts, W. Adolphe. "Confidences Off-Screen." *Motion Picture* 30 (Dec. 1925): 54–55.

609. Robinson, David. "Dunkenfield Meets McGargle; Creation of a Character." *Sight and Sound* 36 (Summer 1967): 125–129.

610. Robinson, Jeffrey. "A Man Named Fields." *National Air Lines 'Aloft'* (Winter 1971-72): 12–14, 54.

611. Rogow, Lee. "High Priests of Martini." *Saturday Review of Literature* 37 (24 April 1954): 19.

612. "Rogue's Progress." *Newsweek* 29 (6 Jan. 1947): 19.

613. Rosten, Leo. "The World of Leo Rosten." *Look* 31-22 (31 Oct. 1967): 12.

Explains a quotation attributed to Fields.

614. St. John-Brenon, Aileen. "Cinema Notes." (Fields in Janice Meredith.) *Theatre* 39 (June 1924): 58.

615. Sanders, Bob. "W. C. Fields." *Southland Sunday* (26 Dec. 1971): 8–11.

Published by *Long Beach Independent-Telegram.*

616. Schuessler, Raymond. "W. C. Fields Gets His Due." *Modern Maturity* 23 (Aug.-Sept. 1980): 64.

617. Sedgwick, Ruth Waterbury. "Chums—Two Stars from the Big Broadcast of 1938." *Stage* 15-4 (Jan 1939): 59.

Fields and Kirsten Flagstad.

618. ________. "William the Conqueror, Alias W. C. Fields." *Stage* 15 (April 1938): 37.

619. Seldes, Gilbert. "Diamond Pin Money." *Photoplay* 52 (Feb. 1938): 23, 85.

620. "Self-Made Curmudgeon." *Time* (17 Oct. 1949): 108, 110, 113.

621. "Shadow Stage: A Review of the New Pictures." *Photoplay* 46 (Sept. 1934): 51.

622. Shlyen, Ben. ed. "Production Index: Features." *Box Office* 29-8 (18 July 1936): 35.
Fields on cover.

623. "Short Pictures—with Sound. The Golf Specialist." *Motion Picture Herald* 102-6 (7 Feb. 1931): 21.

624. "Should Auld Acquaintance Be Forgot—In a Busy World of Fame and Success One Man [Don Dickerman] Finds Time To Pay a Debt of Gratitude." *Radio & Television Mirror* 14 (Sept. 1940): 26–27.
Fields and Rudy Vallee opening night at Dickerman's "Pirates Den" in Hollywood.

625. "Silly Sequences." *Screenland* 36-4 (Feb. 1938): 41.

626. Silver, Gordon R. "Lucky Names: New Names for Old and Perhaps a Life Time of Happy Days in Place of a Destiny of Disaster." *Silver Screen* 8-9 (July 1938): 54–55, 68.

627. Slide, Anthony. "The Collecting Scene." *Films in Review* 31 (Dec. 1981): 629.

628. Smith, Frederick James. "Is His Nose Red? Inside Facts About the Great Fields-McCarthy Vendetta." *Liberty* 14 (4 Sept. 1937): 37–38.

629. Starr, Cecile. "The Film Forum: W. C. Fields: Four Films." *Saturday Review of Literature* 33 (26 Aug. 1950): 28.

630. Steiger, Rod. "W. C. Fields and Me." *TWA Ambassador* (Dec. 1975): 10–12, 34.

631. Sufrin, Mark. "Rod Steiger: W. C. Fields and Me Monument to a Turbulent Career." *Saga* 52 (May 1976): 24–27, 42, 44, 46–47.

632. Sullivan, Ed. "That Lovable Liar: An Appreciation of W. C. Fields and His Gift for Picturesque Exaggeration." *Silver Screen* 5 (Sept. 1935): 14–15, 57–58.

633. Sunlight. "Possibilités. Le sourire de W. C. Fields." *Ciné-Miroir* 598 (18 Sept. 1936): 599.

634. Sutherland, Edward, as told to Scoop Conlon. "W. C. Fields Laughed at Death!" *Hollywood* 25 (Aug. 1936): 29, 58.

635. Svensrud, Lois. "West Coast Chatter: Typical Tidbits and Tidings of Your Favorites Among Hollywood Broadcasters." *Radio Stars* 1 (Aug. 1937): 16–17.

636. "Talkie Tips." (Photo.) *Film Fun* 62 (Sept. 1934): 56.

637. "Talkie Tips." (Photo.) *Film Fun* 63 (May 1935): 56.

638. Taylor, Frank J. "The War of the Juices." *Collier's* 104 (30 Dec. 1939): 24–25, 48.

Photo of Fields posed with a row of juice filled glasses. Serious article about fruit growers, juices, and vitamins.

639. Taylor, Robert Lewis. "Rowdy King of Comedy." *Saturday Evening Post* 221–222 (21 May): 19–21, 70, 72–73, 76, 78; (28 May): 24–25, 113–114, 116, 118, 121; (4 June): 26–27, 112, 115, 117; (11 June): 36–37, 102, 104–106; (18 June): 30, 143–146; (25 June): 30, 55–56, 58, 62; (2 July): 34, 77–80; (9 July 1949): 30, 104–106.

640. ________. "W. C. Fields: His Follies and Fortunes: Condensed from the Book . . . ." *Reader's Digest* 55 (Dec. 1949): 143–162.

641. "Their Stairways to Fame." *Pictureplay* 28 (Aug. 1928): 24.

642. "They Make You Laugh." *Screen Album* (Winter 1939): 26.

643. "They'll Drive You Crazy!" (Photo.) *Film Fun* 59 (Sept. 1933): 48.

644. Thompson, Don. "Stripstuff." *Beautiful Balloons* 144 (Oct. 1982): 42–43.

"Subject: *W. C. Field* [*sic*] comic strip by Frank Smith and James Smart. Review: The *W. C. Fields* strip is awful (this sample is about as funny as it gets.)"

645. Thompson, Herbert. ed. "Tribute to a Grand Film Clown: W. C. Fields, Juggler, Becomes a Film Star." *Film Weekly* 12-299 (6 July 1934): 4–5, 35–36.

646. Thorp, Dunham. "The Up-To-Date Old Timer: W. C. Fields Is an Old Hand at the Comedy Game, Which Accounts for His Perfect Pantomime. He Believes in Keeping Pace with the Public by Presenting Some New Ideas." *Motion Picture Classic* 24 (Sept. 1926): 38–39, 88–89.

647. Top Hat. "Reviews of Previews. Poppy." *Hollywood* 25 (Aug. 1936): 34.

648. "Topics for Gossips." (Photo.) *Silver Screen* 8-9 (July 1938): 15.

649. Townsend, Leo. "Tales from the Redwood: The Fields Explains His Roseate Proboscis, and How an Arch-Fiend Bit Him, and Other Matters." *Radio Stars* 1 (Sept. 1937): 24–25, 76.

650. Tully, Jim. "The Clown Who Juggled Apples. His Audiences Did Not Know Whether to Laugh or Cry." *Photoplay* 45 (Jan. 1934): 60, 108–109.

651. ______. "Clowns Never Laugh—Except for Money, Says W. C. Fields. A Dramatic Close-Up of the Former Vagabond Who Is Now One of the World's Greatest Comedians." *This Week* (6 Sept. 1936): 2, 12.

652. ______. "Let's Laugh at Life with W. C. Fields: The Personal Recitation of a Famous and Eventful Life." *Screenplay* 18 (June 1935): 30–31, 81–83.

653. ______. "My Neighbors." *Motion Picture* 49 (March 1935): 32–33, 77; (April 1935): 40–41, 78.

654. Tupper, Lucy. "Dickens on the Screen." *Films in Review* 10 (March 1959): 146–147.

655. Tynan, Kenneth. "Toby Jug and Bottle." *Sight and Sound* 19 (Feb. 1951): 395–398.

656. "The Two Bills! Both Box Office! Will Rogers, Known to His Pals as 'Bill,' Is Now 'In Old Kentucky.' 'Mr. Micawber' Goes Modern in His New Comedy. What, No Juggling?" *Screenland* 31 (Sept. 1935): 40–41.

657. "Two Boys Trying to Break In. W. C. Fields and Chester Conklin Are Hunting for a Co-Starring Story. They Tried Out These Six Great Dramas Before Jesse Lasky One Day. The Boss Turned 'Em Down and the Boys Are Still Hunting." *Photoplay* 32 (Oct. 1927): 56–57.

658. Underhill, Duncan. "Epic of the [18]80's." *Screen Life* 22-2 (March 1940): 32–33, 91–92.

659. "Une douzaine de jolies filles, cela devrait bien dérider W. C. Fields!" *Cinémonde* 355 (8 Aug. 1935): 614.

660. "Us Trivia." (Photo.) *Us Magazine* (14 Oct. 1980): 78.

661. Van Dyke, Willard. "Cue Salutes Comedian W. C. Fields." *Cue* 39 (28 March 1970): 54–55.

662. Vidal, Jean. "Les films de la Semaine; *Poker Party [Tillie & Gus]*." *Pour Vous* 303 (6 Sept. 1934): 6, 15.

663. "Vogue Spotlight." *Vogue* 114 (1 Nov. 1949): 110.

664. Vreeland, Frank. "Screenland." (Sally of the Sawdust.) *Theatre* 42 (Oct. 1925): 32–33.

665. Walker, Helen Louise. "The Fields You Ought to Know." 44-*Picture Play* 3 (May 1936): 52–53, 64.

666. Walton, Jeff. "The Faces of W. C. Fields." *Funny Business* 1 (Winter 1982): 14–15.

667. Wanger, Walter F. "The Films: Forward from 1941." *Theatre Arts* 25 (Sept. 1941): 631–632.

668. Waterbury, Ruth. "Close Ups and Long Shots." *Photoplay* 53 (April 1939): 8, 14.

669. ________. "The Old Army Game. W. C. Fields, the Overnight Comedy Sensation of 'Sally of the Sawdust' Knows His Stuff." *Photoplay* 28 (Oct. 1925): 68, 101–102.

670. ________. "Studio Defies Precedent: Brings Faithful Reproduction of Classic to Screen." *Movie Mirror* 6 (April 1935): 8.

671. Watts, Richard, Jr. "Authentic Comic Genius: W. C. Fields: His Follies and Fortunes, by Robert Lewis Taylor." *Saturday Review of Literature* 32 (22 Oct. 1949): 26–27.

672. "W. C. Fields." (Biography & photo.) *Moving Picture World* 25 (25 Sept. 1915): 2162.

673. "W. C. Fields and Charlie McCarthy." *This Week* (19 Sept. 1937): 3.
Chase & Sanborn ad.

674. "W. C. Fields, Chief Fun-Maker in the New Earl Carroll Vanities, as Seen by Our Caricaturist Irving Hoffman." *Theatre* 48 (Sept. 1928): 9.

675. "W. C. Fields: Con Man, First Class." *Exploiter* 2-24 (14 June 1970): 20.

676. "W. C. Fields Courtesy of F. Ziegfeld Jr. Appearing in Casino Star Comedies Next Release His Lordship's Dilemma Oct. 3rd." *Motion Picture News* 12 (9 Oct. 1915): 113.

677. "W. C. Fields in the Golf Specialist." *Exhibitors Herald World* 100-8 (25 Aug. 1930): 18.
Name changed to *Motion Picture Herald* 102-1 (3 Jan. 31).

678. "W. C. Fields in 'Man on the Flying Trapeze.'" *Literary Digest* 120 (10 Aug. 1935): 29.

679. "W. C. Fields in 'The Pool Sharks.' All Star Comedy Released Sept. 19th." *Motion Picture News* 12 (18 Sept. 1915): 21.

680. "W. C. Fields Is Alive and Well & Living in Portage, Indiana." *Star* (16 Jan. 1990): 5.

681. "W. C. Fields Just Naturally Looks the Way a Comic Should." *Life* 16 (10 Jan. 1944): 79.

682. "W. C. Fields' Limo Joins Imperial Palace Display." *Cars & Parts* (Aug. 1987): 18.

683. "W. C. Fields." (Obituary.) *Illustrated London News* 210 (4 Jan. 1947): 19.

684. "W. C. Fields." (Photo.) *Memory Lane* 1-88 (June 1980): 32–33.

685. "W. C. Fields." (Photo.) *Movie Classic* 6 (April 1934): 14.

686. "W. C. Fields." (Photo.) *Screen Greats* 1 (Summer 1971): 64.

687. "W. C. Fields." (Photo.) *Stage 12* (Aug. 1935): 24.

688. "W. C. Fields." (Photo.) *Vogue* 170-5 (May 1980): 288.

689. "W. C. Fields Private Art Collection: Caricature of Himself Sent by a Fan." *Photoplay* 51 (Dec. 1937): 45.

690. "W. C. Fields. The Red Nosed, Raspy-Voiced Funnyman, Who Never Gave a Sucker an Even Break, Dies on Christmas Day." *Life* 22 (6 Jan. 1947): 63–64, 77.

691. "W. C. Fields Returns for the Third Time in Poppy." *Newsweek* 7 (20 June 1936): 24.

692. "W. C. Fields Tribute and Co-Stars Appear." *Hollywood Studio Magazine* 13 (March 1980): 4.

693. "W. C. Fields Went on the Wagon Again, Predicted No Good Would Come of It." *Time* 38 (24 Nov. 1941): 66.

694. West, John C. "The Remarkable Rise of A. Pismo Clam." Chicago Daily News—*Panorama* (26 Nov. 1966): 3.

695. ———. "W. C. Fields: The Bubble Still Hasn't Burst." *Los Angeles Times Calendar* (11 Dec. 1966): 77.

696. Westcott, Amory. "Fields For Fun! All About That Laughmaker Everybody Likes—Except Baby Leroy!" *Screenland* 28-4 (Feb. 1934): 56, 96–97.

697. "When a Loon Meets a Lulu." *Pic* 7 (20 Feb. 1940): 16–17.

698. White, David Manning. "My Little Chickadee." *Flashback, Take 1* (April 1972): 23–24.

699. Williams, Whitney. "Fields and Screams!" *Hollywood* 26 (Nov. 1937): 40, 67.

700. Wilson, Elizabeth. "The Mad, Merry Set!" *Screenland* 31 (July 1935): 18–19, 95.

701. Winston, Carl. H. "Martinis for Breakfast." *Ace* 3-2 (Aug. 1959): 3, 10–11, 63–64.

702. Wischnia, Bob. "Me and an Old Juggler Named Bill." *Arizona Magazine* (7 Oct. 1973): 32, 34–35.
Interview with Allen Wood.

703. "World Famous Faces in Action." *Screenland* 38-3 (Jan. 1939): 37.

704. Yarrow, Jack. "The Weird Love Life of W. C. Fields." *Tip-Off* 1 (Oct. 1956): 20–21, 64, 66.

705. Zeitlin, Ida. "Fields Without Hedges." *Screenland* 36 (Jan. 1938): 32–33, 71.

706. ———. "Life Begins at Fifty!" *Screenland* 30 (April 1935): 31, 86–88.

707. ———. "W. C. Fields' Real Life Story." *Screenland* 31 (June): 14–15, 78, 80; (July): 52–53, 82–84; (Aug. 1935): 50–51, 74–75.

708. Zimmerman, P. D. "Great Debunker." *Newsweek* 69 (3 April 1967): 88–89.

Press Books

The following material is in the custody of the Motion Picture Section, Prints and Photographs Division, Reference Department, of the Library of Congress. The material is available for study by scholars in the Motion Picture Section, but may not be reproduced without written permission from the copyright holder. The material is not available for loan.

Each entry below contains copyright registration number, film title, and copyright description.

Press books are paperbound, profusely illustrated, and give information about the movie, cast, credits, and advertising accessories.

709. LP20996. *Janice Meredith.* Synopsis, 2pp.

710. LP21808. *Sally of the Sawdust.* Press Book.

711. LP22094. *That Royale Girl.* Press Book.

712. LP22763. *It's the Old Army Game.* Press Book.

713. LP23265. *So's Your Old Man.* Press Book.

714. LP23606. *The Potters.* Press Book.

715. LP23426. *Running Wild.* Press Book.

716. LP24772. *Two Flaming Youths.* Press Book.

717. LP25031. *Tillie's Punctured Romance.* Press Book.

718. LP1507. *The Golf Specialist.* Dialogue, 8pp.

719. LP2671. *Her Majesty Love.* Synopsis, ½p.

720. LP3140. *Million Dollar Legs.* Press Book.

721. LP3423. *If I Had a Million.* Press Book.

722. LP3695. *The Fatal Glass of Beer.* Dialogue, 7pp.

723. LP3465. *The Dentist.* Dialogue, 8pp.

724. LP3821. *The Pharmacist.* Dialogue, 9pp.

725. LP4038. *The Barber Shop.* Dialogue, 10pp.

726. LP3918. *International House.* Press Book.

727. LP4172. *Tillie and Gus.* Press Book.

728. LP4386. *Alice in Wonderland.* Press Book.

729. LP4470. *Six of a Kind.* Press Book.

730. LP4597. *You're Telling Me.* Press Book.

731. LP4823. *The Old Fashioned Way.* Press Book.

732. LP5037. *Mrs. Wiggs of the Cabbage Patch.* Press Book.

733. LP5135. *It's a Gift.* Press Book.

734. LP5259. *David Copperfield.* Dialogue; cutting continuity.

735. LP5417. *Mississippi.* Press Book.

736. LP5683. *The Man on the Flying Trapeze.* Press Book.

737. LP6442. *Poppy.* Press Book.

738. LP7843. *The Big Broadcast of 1938.* Press Book.

739. LP8671. *You Can't Cheat an Honest Man.* Production data; Synopsis, 5pp.

740. LP9425. *My Little Chickadee.* Synopsis, 7paragraphs.

741. LP10080. *The Bank Dick.* Production data; Synopsis, 4pp.

742. LP10770. *Never Give a Sucker an Even Break.* Synopsis, 2pp. Production data with short review.

743. LP12825. *Sensations of 1945.* Press Book, 3pp. Synopsis, and cutting continuity.

Press books for the following films are not in the Library of Congress Collection: 1.) Pool Sharks; *2.)* His Lordship's Dilemma; *3.)* Fools for Luck; *4.)* How to Break Ninety; Hip Action; *5.)* Hollywood on Parade (B-2); *6.)* Hollywood on Parade (B10); *7.)* Tales of Manhattan; *8.)* Follow the Boys; *9.)* Song of the Open Road.

It is doubtful that press books were issued for the Gaumont films, Pool Sharks *and* His Lordship's Dilemma. *Both were filmed and released to the theaters in less than four weeks, making it nearly impossible to prepare such enhancements. It is quite possible that trade publications were Gaumont's only form of advertisement.*

Press books were issued for Fools for Luck, Follow the Boys, Tales of Manhattan, *and* Song of the Open Road. *It is unlikely that press books were issued for* How to Break Ninety; Hip Action, *or either of the* Hollywood on Parade *releases since all three films were special interest features.*

The Library of Congress Collection also lacks press books for which the copyright office issued registration numbers: 1.) Janice Meredith; *a spectacular film. A press book was issued with a variety of elaborate tie-in materials, such as a program, a herald, and a photo-play edition of the book upon which the film was based. 2.)* The Golf Specialist *is a specialty feature within a series. It is doubtful that a press book was issued. 3.)* Her Majesty Love; *a press book was issued for this film. 4.)* The Fatal Glass of Beer, The Dentist, The Pharmacist, *and* The Barber Shop; *Raymond Rohauer owns the rights to all Mack Sennett shorts, and may be best qualified to determine whether or not press books were issued.* The Barber Shop *is the only film for which lobby cards have been seen by collectors. 5.)* David Copperfield; *The M-G-M press book is one of the most sensational ever issued. It measures 49cm × 35cm; has 19 pages, and 32 leaves in addition to cover illustrations; 6.) Press books were issued for all of the Universal films starring Fields;* You Can't Cheat an Honest Man, My Little Chickadee, The Bank Dick, Never Give a Sucker an Even Break.

One of the most interesting Universal press books is You Can't Cheat an Honest Man. *It is a huge 44cm × 58cm with two pages illustrating the movie memorabilia tie-ins. For Fields' fans there is a greeting card from White & Wyckoff Mfg. Co., Holyoke, Mass., and a W. C. Fields ventriloquist's doll from Effanbee Products, New York, N.Y. The Charlie McCarthy tie-ins are too numerous to list.*

The Fields doll was first used as a tie-in to Paramount's The Big Broadcast of 1938.

Typescripts of Unpublished Dramas

These works by W. C. Fields are contained in the Manuscript Division of the Library of Congress. The date given is the year of copyright. Titles followed by an asterisk are present in more than one version. Pagination is approximate length when there is more than one version. All typescripts are written for the stage.

744. *An Episode on the Links.* 1918. 6pp.

745. *An Episode of Lawn Tennis.* 1918. 4pp.

746. *The Mountain Sweep Steaks.* 1919. 13pp.

747. *Just Before the Battle Mother.* 1919. 19pp.

748. *The Family Ford.** 1919, 1920. 8pp.

749. *An Episode at the Dentists.** 1919, 1926, 1928. 11pp.

750. *The Pullman Sleeper.* 1921. 10pp.

751. *Off to the Country.** 1921, 1922. 6pp.

752. *What a Night!* 1921. 8pp.

753. *The Sport Model.* 1922. 4pp.

754. *The Caledonian Express.* 1922. 5pp.

755. *Ten Thousand People Killed.* 1922. 7pp.

756. *The Sleeping Porch.* 1925. 5pp.

757. *Stolen Bonds.* 1928. 2pp.

758. *My School Days Are Over.* 1928. 2pp.

759. *The Midget Car.* 1930. 5pp.

760. [Mumford, L. Quincy]. *Annual Report of the Librarian of*

Congress for the Fiscal Year Ending June 30, 1969. Washington, D.C.: Library of Congress, 1970. 161pp.

Transfers from the Copyright Office to the manuscript collection included Amos and Andy radio scripts and W. C. Fields vaudeville scripts (44).

In 1973, 749–755 of the typescripts in the Library of Congress collection were published by Ronald Fields in his book W. C. Fields by Himself *(105–137).*

FILMOGRAPHY

761. 19 Sept. 1915. *Pool Sharks.* Gaumont Company. Casino Star Comedies. Director: Edwin Middleton. Cast: W. C. Fields, Bud Ross. 1 reel.

762. 3 Oct. 1915. *His Lordship's Dilemma.* Gaumont Company. Casino Star Comedies. Director: William Haddock. Cast: W. C. Fields, Bud Ross. 1 reel.

This is the first of Fields' lost films.

763. 27 Oct. 1924. *Janice Meredith.* A Cosmopolitan Production distributed by M-G-M. Director: E. Mason Hopper. Cast: Marion Davies, Harrison Ford, W. C. Fields, Macklyn Arbuckle, Joseph Kilgour, George Nash, Tyrone Power, May Vokes, Olin Howard, Hattie Delaro, Spencer Charters, Douglas Stevenson, Helen Worthing. Fields is in one scene as a British Sergeant. Length: 153 minutes.

Complete prints of this film have not been located.

764. 2 Aug. 1925. *Sally of the Sawdust.* A Paramount film distributed by United Artists. Director: D. W. Griffith. Cast: W. C. Fields, Carol Dempster, Alfred Lunt, Erville Anderson, Effie Shannon, Charles Hammond, Roy Applegate, Florence Fair, Marie Shotwell, Glen Anders. Fields is cast as Professor Eustace McGargle. Length: 104 minutes.

This is Fields' first feature length film in a starring role.

765. 7 Dec. 1925. *That Royale Girl.* Famous Players-Lasky Corporation distributed by Paramount. Director: D. W. Griffith. Cast: W. C. Fields, Carol Dempster, Harrison Ford, James Kirkwood, Paul Everton, Kathleen Chambers, George Rigas, Florence Auer, Ida Waterman, Alice Laidley, Dorothea Love, Dore Davidson, Frank Allworth, Bobby Watson. Fields is cast as the Father of Joan Daisy Royle. Length: 114 minutes.

Prints of this film are not known to exist.

766. 24 May 1926. *It's the Old Army Game.* Famous Players-Lasky Corporation distributed by Paramount. Director: Edward Sutherland. Cast: W. C. Fields, Louise Brooks, Blanche Ring, William Gaxton, Mary Foy, Mickey Bennett. Fields is cast as Elmer Prettywillie. Length: 70 minutes.

767. 25 Oct. 1926. *So's Your Old Man.* Famous Players-Lasky Corporation distributed by Paramount. Director: Gregory La Cava. Cast: W. C. Fields, Alice Joyce, Charles Rogers, Kittins Reichert, Marcia Harris, Julia Ralph, Frank Montgomery, Jerry Sinclair. Fields is cast as Samuel Bisbee. Length: 67 minutes.

768. 31 Jan. 1927. *The Potters.* Famous Players-Lasky Corporation distributed by Paramount. Director: Fred Newmeyer. Cast: W. C. Fields, Mary Alden, Ivy Harris, Jack Egan, Richard Gallagher, Joseph Smiley, Bradley Barker. Fields is cast as Pa Potter. Length: 71 minutes.

Prints of this film are not known to exist.

769. 20 Aug. 1927. *Running Wild.* Famous Players-Lasky Corporation distributed by Paramount. Director: Gregory La Cava. Cast: W. C. Fields, Mary Brian, Claude Buchanan, Marie Shotwell, Barney Rasken, Fred Burton, J. M. Bennett, Frank Evans, Edward Roseman, Thomas Madden. Fields is cast as Elmer Finch. Length: 68 minutes.

770. 17 Dec. 1927. *Two Flaming Youths.* A Paramount production. Director: John Waters. Cast: W. C. Fields, Chester Conklin, Mary Brian, Jack Luden, George Irving, Cissy Fitzgerald, Jimmy Quinn. Fields is cast as Gabby Gilfoil. Length: 55 minutes.

Prints of this film are not known to exist.

771. 3 March 1928. Al Christie presents *Tillie's Punctured Romance.* A Paramount Picture. Director: Edward Sutherland. Cast: W. C. Fields, Chester Conklin, Louise Fazenda, Mack Swain, Doris Hill, Grant Withers, Tom Kennedy, Babe London, Billy Platt, Kalla Pasha, Mickey Bennett, Mike Rafetto, Baron von Dobeneck. Fields is cast as "The Ringmaster." Length: 57 minutes.

Prints of this film are not known to exist. Advertising tie-ins: Photoplay edition of original story. See item 374 in bibliography.

772. 7 May 1928. *Fools for Luck.* A Paramount production. Director: Charles F. Reisner. Cast: W. C. Fields, Chester Conklin, Sally Blane, Jack Luden, Mary Alden, Arthur Housman, Robert Dudley, Martha Maddox. Fields is cast as Richard Whitehead. Length: 60 minutes.

Prints of this film are not known to exist.

773. 22 Aug. 1930. Series Title: *Broadway Headliners.* Film Title: *The Golf Specialist.* A Radio Pictures production distributed by RKO [Radio-Keith-Orpheum]. Director: Monte Brice. Cast: W. C. Fields, others unnamed. Fields is cast as Effingham Bellweather. Length: 20 minutes.

This is Fields' first sound film. Script by W. C. Fields.

774. 26 Dec. 1931. *Her Majesty Love.* Warner Brothers-First National. Director: William Dieterle. Cast: W. C. Fields, Marilyn Miller, Ben Lyon, Chester Conklin, Ford Sterling, Leon Errol, Harry Stubbs, Maude Eburne, Harry Holman, Ruth Hall, William Irving, Mae Madison, Clarence Wilson, Virginia Sale. Fields is cast as Bela Toerrek. Length: 75 minutes.

Advertising tie-ins: Sheet music; See Stubblebine's *Cinema Sheet Music*, #2073. Fields stopped using his clip-on moustache after this film was completed. He briefly resumed the use of clip-on moustaches in *The Big Broadcast of 1938* and, *You Can't Cheat an Honest Man.*

775. 8 July 1932. *Million Dollar Legs.* A Paramount production. Director: Edward Cline. Cast: Jack Oakie, W. C. Fields, Susan Fleming, Lyda Roberti, Andy Clyde, Ben Turpin, Hugh Herbert, George Barbier, Dickie Moore, Billie Gilbert, John Sinclair, Vernon Dent, Teddy Hart, Sam Adams, Irving Bacon, Ben Taggart, Hank Mann, Chick Collins, Sid Saylor. Fields is cast as "The President" of Klopstokia. Length: 64 minutes.

776. 2 Dec. 1932. *If I Had a Million.* A Paramount production. Director: Norman Taurog. Cast: W. C. Fields, Alison Skipworth, Richard Bennett, Cecilia Cunningham. Paramount all-star cast in a series of episodes linked by one million dollar inheritances. Fields is cast as Rollo in the Road Hog episode [10 minutes]. Overall film length: 88 minutes.

Advertising tie-in: Photoplay edition of original story. See item 190 in bibliography. *Windfall* later became the basis of the television production *The Millionaire.*

777. 9 Dec. 1932. *The Dentist.* A Mack Sennett Star Comedy. Paramount. Director: Leslie Pearce. Cast: W. C. Fields, Babe Kane, Elise Cavanna. Fields is cast as "The Dentist." Length: 20 minutes.

Script by W. C. Fields.

778. 3 March 1933. *The Fatal Glass of Beer.* A Mack Sennett Star Comedy. Paramount. Director: Clyde Bruckman. Cast: W. C. Fields, Rosemary Theby, George Chandler, Richard Cramer, George Moran. Fields is cast as Mr. Snavely. Length: 20 minutes.

Script by W. C. Fields.

779. 21 April 1933. *The Pharmacist.* A Mack Sennett Star Comedy. Paramount. Director: Arthur Ripley. Cast: W. C. Fields, Elise Cavanna, Babe Kane, Grady Sutton, Lorena Carr. Fields is cast as Mr. Dilweg. Length: 20 minutes.

Script by W. C. Fields.

780. 2 June 1933. *International House.* A Paramount production. Director: Edward Sutherland. Cast: W. C. Fields, Peggy Hopkins Joyce, Bèla Lugosi, Stuart Erwin, Sari Maritza, George Burns, Gracie Allen, Edmund Breese, Lumsden Hare, Franklin Pangborn, Harrison Greene, Henry Sedley, James Wong, Sterling Holloway, Rudy Vallee, Stoopnagle and Bud, Cab Calloway, Baby Rose Marie. Fields is cast as Professor Quail. Length: 70 minutes.

Advertising tie-in: Sheet music; See Stubblebine #2373.

781. 24 June 1933. Series Title: *How to Break Ninety.* Film Title: *Hip Action* No. 3. Warner Brothers film released by Vitaphone Corporation. Director: George E. Marshall. Cast: W. C. Fields, Bobby Jones, Warner Oland, William B. Davidson. Length: 8 minutes. Overall film length: 144 minutes.

See bibliography #242 (Everson page 97).

782. 28 July 1933. *The Barber Shop.* A Mack Sennett Star Comedy. Paramount. Director: Arthur Ripley. Cast: W. C. Fields, Elise Cavanna, Dagmar Oakland, Harry Watson. Fields cast as Cornelius O'Hare. Length 20 minutes.
Script by W. C. Fields.

783. 8 Sept. 1933. *Hollywood on Parade* (B-2). Paramount. Director: Louis Lewyn. Cast: W. C. Fields and 14 other Paramount players. Exploitation film used to show off Paramount talent. Length: 1 reel.

784. 13 Oct. 1933. *Tillie and Gus.* Paramount. Director: Francis Martin. Cast: W. C. Fields, Allison Skipworth, Baby LeRoy, Jacqueline Wells, Clifford Jones, Clarence Wilson, George Barbier, Barton MacLane, Edgar Kennedy, Master Williams, Robert McKenzie. Fields is cast as Augustus Winterbottom. Length: 58 minutes.

785. 22 Dec. 1933. *Alice in Wonderland.* Paramount. Director: Norman McLeod. Cast: Charlotte Henry, W. C. Fields, Roscoe Ates, William Austin, Gary Cooper, Jack Duffy, Leon Errol, Louise Fazenda, Skeets Gallagher, Alec B. Francis, Cary Grant, Lillian Harmer, Raymond Hatton, Sterling Holloway, Baby LeRoy, Billy Barty, Edward Everett Horton, Roscoe Karns, Mae Marsh, Lucian Littlefield, Polly Moran, Jack Oakie, Edna Mae Oliver, George Ovey, May Robson, Charlie Ruggles, Allison Skipworth, Ned Sparks, Jackie Searle, Ford Sterling, Jacqueline Wells. Fields is cast as Humpty Dumpty. Length: 90 minutes.
Advertising tie-ins to this film include four Photoplay editions of the original story. See numbers 209, 210, 378, 379 in bibliography. Sheet music; see Stubblebine #78. Other items consisted of photos, soap cakes of film characters, hats, Alice dolls, novelty figures in plaster and metal, such as bookends and irons. Alice toys, costumes, Alice head bands, Alice tea sets, color effect slides, jewelry tokens, and Alice picture cut-outs.

786. 9 Feb. 1934. *Six of a Kind.* Paramount. Director: Leo McCarey. Cast: W. C. Fields, Alison Skipworth, Charlie Ruggles, Mary Boland, George Burns, Gracie Allen, Bradley Page, William J. Kelly, Grace Bradley, Tammany Young,

James Burke, Dick Rush, Walter Long, Leo Willis, Lew Kelly, Al P. James, Paul Tead, George Pearce, Florence Enright, Verna Hillie, William Augustin, Kathleen Burke, Irving Bacon, Phil Dunham, Marty Faust, Neal Burns, Lee Phelps. Fields is cast as Sheriff "Honest John" Hoxley. Length: 65 minutes.

787. 6 April 1934. *You're Telling Me.* Paramount. Director: Earle Kenton. Cast: W. C. Fields, Louise Carter, Joan Marsh, Larry "Buster" Crabbe, Adrienne Ames, Kathleen Howard, James Kenton, Robert MacKenzie, George Irving, Jerry Stewart, Dell Henderson, Nora Cecil, George MacQuarrie, John M. Sullivan, Elise Cavanna, Tammany Young, Vernon Dent, Alfred Delcambre, Frederic Sullivan, William Robyns, Harold Berquist, Lee Phelps, Frank O'Connor, Florence Enright, Isabelle LaMal, Edward LeSaint, James Morton, Billy Engle, George Ovey, Al Hart, Hal Craig, Dorothy Bay. Fields is cast as Samuel Bisbee. Length: 66 minutes.

Advertising tie-in: Sheet music; see Stubblebine #6152.

788. 27 April 1934. *Paramount on Parade* (B-10). Paramount. Director: Louis Lewyn. W. C. Fields and two dozen other Paramount players. Exploitation film used to show off Paramount talent. Length: 1 reel.

See bibliography #307 (Maltin page 84).

789. 13 July 1934. *The Old Fashioned Way.* Paramount. Director: William LeBaron. Cast: W. C. Fields, Judith Allen, Joe Morrison, Jan Duggan, Nora Cecil, Baby LeRoy, Jack Mulhall, Joe Mills, Samuel Ethridge, Emma Ray, Ruth Marion, Del Henderson, Clarence Wilson, Richard Carle, Otis Harlan, Tammany Young, Dorothy Ray, Oscar Smith, Maxine Hicks, Lew Kelly, Davidson Clark, Edward LeSaint. Fields is cast as "The Great McGonigle" throughout the film, and as Squire Cribbs in the cast of *The Drunkard.* Length: 66 minutes.

Screenplay is based on an original story by Charles Bogle (W. C. Fields). Advertising tie-in: Sheet music; see Stubblebine #3686.

790. 19 Oct. 1934. *Mrs. Wiggs of the Cabbage Patch.* Paramount.

Director: Norman Taurog. Cast: W. C. Fields, Pauline Lord, ZaSu Pitts, Evalyn Venable, Kent Taylor, Charles Middleton, Donald Meek, Jimmy Butler, George Breakston, Edith Fellows, Virginia Weidler, Carmencita Johnson, George Reed, Mildred Grover, Arthur Housman, Walter Walker, Sam Flint, James Robinson, Bentley Hewlett, Edward Tamblin, Al Shaw, Sam Lee, Del Henderson, George Pearce, Lillian Elliott, Earl Pingree. Fields is cast as Mr. Stubbins. Length: 80 minutes.

Advertising tie-in: Photoplay edition of original story. See bibliography #333.

791. 30 Nov. 1934. *It's a Gift.* Paramount. Director: Norman McLeod. Cast: W. C. Fields, Baby LeRoy, Tammany Young, Jean Rouverol, Tom Bupp, Julian Madison, Kathleen Howard, Morgan Wallace, Charles Sellon, Josephine Whittell, Diana Lewis, T. Roy Barnes, Spencer Charters, Guy Usher, Del Henderson, Jerry Mandy, James Burke, William Tooker, Edith Kingdon, Patsy O'Byrne, Billy Engle. Fields cast as Harold Bissonette. Length: 73 minutes.

Screenplay based on original story by J. P. McEvoy, and Charles Bogle (W. C. Fields).

792. 13 Jan. 1935. *David Copperfield.* Metro-Goldwyn-Mayer. Director: George Cukor. Cast: W. C. Fields, Freddie Bartholomew, Frank Lawton, Lionel Barrymore, Maureen O'Sullivan, Madge Evans, Edna May Oliver, Lewis Stone, Elizabeth Allan, Roland Young, Basil Rathbone, Elsa Lanchester, Jean Cadell, Jessie Ralph, Lennox Pawle, Violet Kemble-Cooper, Una O'Connor, John Buckler, Hugh Williams, Ivan Simpson, Herbert Mundin, Fay Chaldecott, Florine McKinney, Marilyn Knowlden, Harry Beresford, Hugh Walpole, Mabel Colcord, Renee Gadd. Fields is cast as Wilkins Micawber. Length: 133 minutes.

Advertising tie-ins: A Big Little Book and three Photoplay editions of the original story. See bibliography numbers 230, 231, 232, 233.

793. 22 March 1935. *Mississippi.* Paramount. Director: Edward Sutherland. Cast: W. C. Fields, Bing Crosby, Joan Bennett, Queenie Smith, Gail Patrick, Claude Gillingwater, Sr., John

Miljan, Edward Pawley, Fred Kohler, Sr., Five Cabin Kids, John Larkin, Libby Taylor, Theresa Conover, Paul Hurst, Jean Rouverol, Ann Sheridan, Harry Meyers, Charles L. King, Mildred Stone, Mary Ellen Brown, J. P. McGowan, Eddie Sturges, George Lloyd, Al Richmond, Francis McDonald, Stanley Andrews, Harry Cody. Fields is cast as Commodore Jackson. Length: 80 minutes.

Advertising tie-in: Sheet music; See Stubblebine #3329.

794. 26 July 1935. *Man on the Flying Trapeze.* Paramount. Director: Clyde Bruckman. Cast: W. C. Fields, Mary Brian, Kathleen Howard, Carlotta Monti, Grady Sutton, Vera Lewis, Lucien Littlefield, Oscar Apfel, Lew Kelly, Tammany Young, Walter Brennan, Arthur Aylesworth, Harry Ekezian, Tor Johnson, David Clyde, Mickey Bennett, Lorin Baker, Dorothy Thompson, Pat O'Mally, Sarah Edwards, James Flavin, Edward Gargan. Fields is cast as Ambrose Wolfinger. Length: 65 minutes.

Advertising tie-in: Sheet music; See Stubblebine #3136.

795. 19 June 1936. *Poppy.* Paramount. Director: Edward Sutherland. Cast: W. C. Fields, Rochelle Hudson, Richard Cromwell, Granville Bates, Catherine Doucet, Lynne Overman, Maude Eburne, Bill Wolfe, Adrian Morris, Rosalind Keith, Ralph Remley, Tammany Young, Dell Henderson, Wade Boteler, Tom Herbert, Cyril Ring, Jack Baxley, Harry Wagner, Frank Sully, Eddie C. Waller, Dewey Robinson, Tom Kennedy, Nora Cecil, Gertrude Sutton, Grace Goodall, Ada May Moore, Jerry Bergen, Doc Sone, Malcolm Waite, Dick Rush, Charles McMurphy. Fields is cast as Professor Eustace McGargle. Length: 75 minutes.

Advertising tie-ins: Flip Book (photos) and sheet music: See Stubblebine #4024.

796. 18 Feb. 1938. *The Big Broadcast of 1938.* Paramount. Director: Mitchell Leisen. Cast: W. C. Fields, Shirley Ross, Martha Raye, Dorothy Lamour, Bob Hope, Lynne Overman, Ben Blue, Lief Erikson, Grace Bradley, Rufe Davis, Patricia Wilder, Lionel Pape, Dorothy Howe, Russell Hicks, Billy Daniels, Michael Brooks, Jack Hubbard, Leonid Kinsky, Stanley King, Rex Moore, Bernard Punsley, Don Marion,

Irving Bacon, Wally Maher, Rebecca Wassem, James Craig, Kirsten Flagstad, Tito Guizar, Shep Fields and orchestra. Fields is cast as two brothers: T. Frothingell Bellows and S. B. Bellows. Length: 97 minutes.

Advertising tie-ins: Effanbee's W. C. Fields ventriloquist doll and sheet music; See Stubblebine #400.

797. 17 Feb. 1939. *You Can't Cheat an Honest Man.* Universal. Director: George E. Marshall. Cast: W. C. Fields, Edgar Bergen, Charlie McCarthy, Mortimer Snerd, Constance Moore, Mary Forbes, Thurston Hall, Grady Sutton, Princess Baba, John Arledge, Charles Coleman, Edward Brophy, Arthur Hohl, Blacaman, Eddie Anderson, Ferris Taylor, James Bush, Ivan Lebedeff, Bill Wolfe. Fields is cast as Larson E. Whipsnade. Length: 76 minutes.

Original story by Charles Bogle (W. C. Fields). Advertising tie-ins: W. C. Fields greeting card by White & Wyckoff Mfg. Co., and Effanbee's W. C. Fields ventriloquist doll, again. Effanbee's Charlie McCarthy doll, coloring book, etc.

798. 9 Feb. 1940. *My Little Chickadee.* Universal. Director: Edward Cline. Cast: W. C. Fields, Mae West, George Moran, Joseph Calleia, Dick Foran, Margaret Hamilton, Si Jenks, Gene Austin, Bill Wolfe, Russell Hall, Otto Heimel, Eddie Butler, Bing Conley, Fuzzy Knight, Anne Nagel, Ruth Donnelly, Willard Robinson, Donald Meek, William B. Davidson, Addison Richards, Jackie Searle, Fay Adler, Jan Duggan, Morgan Wallace, Wade Boteler, Harlan Briggs, Jeff Conlon, John Kelly, Walter McGrail, Otto Hoffman, Billy Benedict, Delmar Watson, Chester Gan, George Melford, Lita Chevret, Bud Harris, Bob McKenzie, James Morton, Joe Whitehead, Slim Gaut, Lloyd Ingraham, George Billings, Ben Hall, Charles McMurphy, Dick Rush, Hank Bell, Buster Slaven, Danny Jackson, Lane Chandler, Charles Hart, Jack Roper, Alan Bridge, Eddie Hearn, Mark Anthony. Fields is cast as Cuthbert J. Twillie. Length: 83 minutes.

Original screenplay by W. C. Fields and Mae West. Advertising tie-in: Sheet music; See Stubblebine #3482.

799. 29 Nov. 1940. *The Bank Dick.* Universal. Director: Edward Cline. Cast: W. C. Fields, Grady Sutton, Bill Wolfe, Cora

Witherspoon, Una Merkel, Evelyn Del Rio, Jessie Ralph, Franklin Pangborn, Shemp Howard, Richard Purcell, Russell Hicks, Pierre Watkin, Al Hill, Kay Sutton, George Moran, Jack Norton, Pat West, Reed Hadley, Heather Wilde, Harlan Briggs, Bill Alston, Malinda Boss. Fields is cast as Egbert Sousé. Length: 74 minutes.

Original screenplay by Mahatma Kane Jeeves (W. C. Fields).

800. 10 Oct. 1941. *Never Give a Sucker an Even Break.* Universal. Director: Edward Cline. Cast: W. C. Fields, Gloria Jean, Billy Lenhart, Kenneth Brown, Anne Nagel, Carlotta Monti, Franklin Pangborn, Leon Errol, Mona Barrie, Margaret Dumont, Susan Miller, Charles Lang, Irving Bacon, Claud Allister, Leon Belasco, Emil Van Horn, Billy Wayne, Minerva Urecal, Jody Gilbert, Al Hill, William Gould, Emmett Vogan, Jack Lipson, Dave Willock, Duke York, Eddie Bruce, Lloyd Ingraham, James Morton, Dick Alexander, Kathryn Sheldon, Irene Colman, Frank Austin, Frances Morris, Jack Roper, Emma Tansey, William Alston, Charles McMurphy, James Sullivan. Fields is cast as himself, aka "The Great Man." Length: 70 minutes.

Original story by Otis Criblecoblis (W. C. Fields).

801. 30 Oct. 1942. *Tales of Manhattan.* Twentieth Century—Fox. Director: Julien Duvivier. Cast: W. C. Fields, Margaret Dumont, Phil Silvers, Elinor Van Der Veer, Gibson Gowland, Jerry Bergen, Dot Farley, Marcel Dalio, Chester Clute, Julia Griffith. An all star cast in a series of episodes linked by a tail coat. Fields is cast as Professor Poindexter Pothlewhistle [9 minutes]. Overall film length: 118 minutes.

The Fields episode was cut from the final version of the film. The nine minute clip is now available on video tape. Advertising tie-in: Sheet music; See Stubblebine #5228.

802. 5 May 1944. *Follow the Boys.* Universal. Director: Edward Sutherland. Cast: George Raft, Vera Zorina, Charles Grapewin, Grace MacDonald, Charles Butterworth, George Macready, Elizabeth Patterson, Theodor von Eltz, Regis Toomey, Ramsey Ames, Spooks, Bill Wolfe, and dozens of guest stars including W. C. Fields. He portrays himself in a short opening scene and later in the film Fields does his pool routine. Length: 118 minutes.

Advertising tie-in: Sheet music; See Stubblebine #1519.

803. 21 June 1944. *Song of the Open Road.* United Artists. Director: S. Sylvan Simon. Cast: Jane Powell, W. C. Fields, Edgar Bergen, Charlie McCarthy, Bonita Granville, Peggy O'Neill, Jackie Moran, Bill Christy, Reginald Denny, Regis Toomey, Rose Hobart, Sig Arno, Irene Tedro, Par Starling, Hugh Beaumont, Sammy Kaye orchestra, The Condon Brothers, Hollywood Canteen Kids, Lipham Four, Chuck Faulkner Band, Catron and Pop. Fields guest appearance as himself. Length: 93 minutes.

Advertising tie-in: Sheet music; See Stubblebine #4868.

804. 30 June 1944. *Sensations of 1945.* United Artists. Director: Andrew L. Stone. Cast: Eleanor Powell, Dennis O'Keefe, C. Aubrey Smith, Eugene Pallette, Lyle Talbot, Hubert Castle, W. C. Fields, Sophie Tucker, Dorothy Donegan, Cab Calloway and Band, Woody Herman and Band. W. C. Fields in a guest appearance as himself. Length: 87 minutes.

Advertising tie-in: Sheet music; See Stubblebine #4578.

CARTOONS AND COMIC STRIPS

From 1934 to 1953 the following 18 film cartoons were produced with W. C. Fields' characterizations, physical likeness and or voice. Warner Bros. produced ten, Disney produced three, Columbia produced two, while Paramount, Twentieth Century–Fox, and Universal each produced one.

805. Dec. 10, 1934. Universal. *Toyland Premier.*

806. Dec. 14, 1935. Disney. *Broken Toys.*

807. Jan. 4, 1936. Disney. *Mickey's Polo Team.*

808. Aug. 29, 1936. Warner Bros. *At Your Service Madam.*

809. Oct. 19, 1936. Warner Bros. *Hollywood Capers.*

810. Nov. 28, 1936. Warner Bros. *The Coo-Coo Nut Grove.*

811. Feb. 6, 1937. Warner Bros. *Porky's Road Race.*

812. Dec. 4, 1937. Warner Bros. *The Woods Are Full of Coo-Coos.*

813. Dec. 18, 1937. Columbia Pictures. *Hollywood Picnic.*

814. April 2, 1938. Warner Bros. *A Star Is Hatched.*

815. June 25, 1938. Warner Bros. *Have You Got Any Castles?*

816. Sept. 10, 1938. Warner Bros. *Cracked Ice.*

817. Dec. 23, 1938. Disney. *Mother Goose Goes Hollywood.*

818. July 6, 1940. Warner Bros. *Little Blabbermouse.*

819. Dec. 21, 1940. Warner Bros. *Shop, Look, and Listen.*

820. Jan. 23, 1942. Columbia Pictures. *A Hollywood Detour.*

821. Nov. 28, 1947. Paramount/Famous. *The Babysitter.*

822. May ??, 1953. 20th Century–Fox/Terrytoons. *Featherweight Champ.*

823. The following article was written by Bill Blackbeard, founder of the San Francisco Academy of Comic Art, and series editor of the 22 volume *Classic American Comic Strips.* We gratefully acknowledge permission of Jud Hurd, and *Cartoonist Profiles* to reprint same.

> Fields was only once identified by name in a strip, to my present knowledge, and that was in what appears to be his first limning in the comics—Frank Hoban's *Jerry on the Job* for 9/25/16, in the *New York Evening Journal*. . . . Apparently overlooked by Merrill Blosser, Walter Berndt, and Carl Ed, when those cartoonists took their strip characters to Hollywood or mixed them with real movie folk at various times between 1910 and 1932. Fields made his next strip appearance a decade later in Ray McGill's little-known hearst strip, *Brodie Betts*. . . . Not too notably Fieldsian in his first days in the strip, McGill's *Betts* quickly acquired Fields' stage and screen characteristics on [*sic*] the 1926 period in almost every respect except height. Julian Ollendorf made up for that ten years further on by introducing the Fields figure unmistakably as his slapstick comic, Cluck, in his 1935 *Olly of the Movies,* another rare strip. Most memorably, of course, Allen Saunders and Elmer Woggon included Fields as a major character virtually from the start of their *Big Chief Wahoo* strip, caricaturing Fields broadly at first in 1936, then relimning him much more closely, in keeping with the growing "realism" of the strip, a half decade later in 1941. Fields himself was aware of most of his strip appearances, particularly delighting in the later *Wahoo* representations. (In fact, Fields' initial entry scene in *My Little Chickadee* was clearly derived from his 1936 entry in the *Wahoo* strip,. . . .)
>
> Fields posed for cartoonists more than once, among them Harry Hershfield and Jim Lowery (of the *Chicago Tribune*).
>
> Fields own cartoon work, although rarely seen in print, was well represented by a self-portrait he sketched for the *Philadelphia Ledger* during a stage appearance in that city in 1917.

One of the earliest of Fields' self-caricatures is in Tibbles' Magician's Handbook, *1901, while many other Fields drawings are reprinted in* W. C. Fields by Himself. . . *edited by Ronald Fields.*

Fields maintained an active interest in cartooning throughout his life, and often drew caricatures and objects at the top of his letters, on stage skits, and on film scripts. He was known to create greeting cards for his friends.

The popularity of the Big Chief Wahoo *comic strip prompted Whitman Publishing Co., Racine, Wisconsin, to publish three* Wahoo *titles as Big Little Books; #1443 in 1938, and #1483 in 1940. The third title did not include the Fields character.*

These were followed by Big Chief Wahoo *comic books in 1942, and were published by Eastern Color Print. A total of 23 issues were printed. The first issue consisted of newspaper reprints of the* Wahoo *comic strips. Steve Roper was introduced in the second issue of the comic books, while Fields' character "The Great Gutso" appeared in only the first five issues of the comics.*

824. Lowery, Lawrence F. *The Collector's Guide to Big Little Books and Similar Books.* Danville, California: Educational Research, c1981. pp.378, [2].

Cover statement: 400 pages. BLB's based on WCF's films on pages 37, 54, 194, 200, 214.

825. Overstreet, Robert M. *The Comic Book Price Guide.* 1973. Books from 1933—present included. Catalogue and price list. Illustrated. Cleveland, Tennessee: The Author, c1973. pp. 399, [1].

Big Chief Wahoo on p. 53.

MUSIC AND RECORDINGS

Film Sheet Music

826. Abbott, Mary Allen. *A Study Guide to the Critical Appreciation of the Photoplay Version of Charles Dickens' Novel* David Copperfield. Newark, New Jersey: National Council of Teachers of English, 1935. 20pp.

A special musical accompaniment was arranged for the film by Dr. William Axt. Fields played Micawber and sang in this film. Critics raved about the film's realism. Fields' portrayal earned him great respect as a legitimate actor.

827. Mullen, Sarah McLean. *Study Guide. Lewis Carroll's Classic of Nonsense* Alice in Wonderland. Published by Committee on Photoplay Appreciation. Newark, New Jersey: National Council of Teachers of English, 1933. 26pp.

The music is an integral part of the picture describing the characters, interpreting the emotions, enhancing the dramatization throughout. Fields' voice was instantly recognizable in his role as Humpty Dumpty.

828. Stubblebine, Donald J. *Cinema Sheet Music: A Comprehensive Listing of Published Film Music from* Squaw Man *(1914) to* Batman *(1989).* Jefferson, North Carolina: McFarland, 1991. 629pp.

This is an indispensable reference work for everyone interested in sheet music. There are 14 entries for sheet music from W. C. Fields' films: p. 6, #78 *Alice in Wonderland;* p. 31, #400 *Big Broadcast of 1938*; p. 114, #1519 *Follow the Boys*; p. 156, #2073 *Her Majesty Love*; p. 178, #2373 *International House*; p. 234, #3136 *Man on the Flying Trapeze;* p. 247,

#3329 *Mississippi;* p. 258, #3482 *My Little Chickadee*; p. 273, #3686 *Old Fashioned Way, The*; p. 298, #4024 *Poppy*; p. 337, #4578 *Sensations of 1945*; p. 359, #4868 *Song of the Open Road*; p. 387, #5228 *Tales of Manhattan*; p. 454, #6152 *You're Telling Me.*

Phonograph Records

(in Chronological Order)

829. W. C. Fields. *"The Day I Drank a Glass of Water." "The Temperance Lecture."* Written and directed by Bill Morrow. Variety Records, Album V-101. c1946.

Three 78 rpm records (6 sides). *The Temperance Lecture,* Part 1 (F1212), Part 2 (F1213), Part 3 (F1214), Part 4 (F1215). *The Day I Drank a Glass of Water,* Part 1 (F1216), Part 2, (F1217).

Inside front cover of album has "The story of my life" by W. C. Fields (with photo).

830. ________. *Temperance Lecture.* Jay Records, Album 2001, c1951.

One 33⅓ rpm record (2 sides). *Temperance Lecture,* 2001-A. *The Day I Drank a Glass of Water,* 2001-B.

831. ________. *Original and Authentic Recordings by the Great W. C. Fields.* Blue Thumb, Album S-3. circa 1966.

One 33⅓ rpm record (2 sides). Same material as Jay Records.

832. ________. *His Only Recording. The Temperance Lecture. The Day I Drank a Glass of Water. Plus 8 Songs by Mae West.* Proscenium, Album 22. 1968.

One 33⅓ rpm record (2 sides). Side 1, PR 22-A: W. C. Fields recording. Side 2, PR 22-B: Mae West songs.

833. ________. *W. C. Fields. The Original Voice Tracks from His Movies.* Narration by Gary Owens. Decca Records, Album DL 79164. n.d. [circa 1968].

One 33⅓ rpm record (2 sides). Each album was issued with a small poster of Fields; three different posters were available from Decca. Sound tracks were taken from the following films: The Bank Dick, The Big Broadcast of 1938, If I Had a Million, It's a Gift, Million Dollar Legs, Mississippi, My Little Chickadee, Never Give a Sucker an Even Break, The Old Fashioned Way, Poppy, Six of a Kind, Tillie & Gus, You Can't Cheat an Honest Man, You're Telling Me. Side one: The Philosophy of W. C. Fields; The Sound of W. C. Fields; The Rascality of W. C. Fields; The Chicanery of W. C. Fields. Side two: W. C. Fields, the Braggart and Teller of Tall Tales; The Spirit of W. C. Fields; W. C. Fields, a Man Against Children, Motherhood, Fatherhood, and Brotherhood; W. C. Fields, Creator of Weird Names.

Reissued by MCA, Album 2073.

834. ________. *The Great Radio Comedians. W. C. Fields. Burns & Allen.* Doubleday & Co., Columbia Special Products. CSM 7899. 1970.

One 33⅓ rpm record (one side). Issued with Jim Harmon's book, *The Great Radio Comedians.*

835. ________. *"Hollywood Is on the Air."* Radio programs of the 1930s and 1940s promoting musical films of the era. Radiola, Album 2MR 1718. 1972.

Two 33⅓ rpm records (four sides). Side 17B: *The Big Broadcast of 1938.* Sides 17A, 18A, 18B have no Fields material.

836. ________. *Lux Radio Theatre. Cecil B. DeMille Presents W. C. Fields.* Poppy. An Original Radio Broadcast. A George Garabedian Production. Mark 56 Records, Album 595. 1972.

One 33⅓ rpm record (2 sides).

837. ________. *Rich Little as W. C. Fields for President.* Edited and Directed by Michael M. Taylor. Script by W. C. Fields. Caedmon Records, Album TC 9101. 1972.

One 33⅓ rpm record (2 sides). Recitation of material from the book.

838. ________. *His Only Recording.* The Temperance Lecture. *The Day I Drank a Glass of Water. Plus Eight Songs by Mae West.* American Album 120. Album AAT 120. 1973.

One 33⅓ rpm record (2 sides). Same material as Proscenium, Album 22.

839. ________. *Mae West & W. C. Fields. Side by Side.* Harmony; a product of Columbia Records. Album HS 11405. n.d.

One 33⅓ rpm record (2 sides). Side 1: Mae West [5] songs. Songs are not the same as Proscenium or American albums. Side 2: W. C. Fields, *The Temperance Lecture, Promotions Unlimited,* and *The Pharmacist.*

840. ________. *Original Radio Broadcasts* with narrative introductions by W. C. Fields, Jr. A George Garabedian Production. Mark 56 Records, Album 571. 1973.

One 33⅓ rpm record (2 sides). Side 1: Introduction by Fields, Jr., *The Pharmacist.* Side 2: Commentary by Fields, Jr., *Promotions Unlimited.* This album was released three times with two different album jackets: a.) Standard Oil Company of California presents. . .; b.) Coca Cola. Nostalgia . . . with regular album. c.) Coca Cola. Nostalgia . . . with a picture disk album. Side one: Coke advertisement; Side two: has 24 cm Fields photo from *Sally of the Sawdust.*

841. ________. *From His Personal Collection. W. C. Fields Festival. "Poppy."* Produced by Bruce Lundvall, Ted Joyce, et al. Columbia, Album KC 33253. 1974.

One 33⅓ rpm record (2 sides). Same material as Mark 56, Album 595.

842. ________. *From His Personal Collection. The Further Adventures of Larson E. Whipsnade and Other Taradiddles.* Produced by Bruce Lundvall, Ted Joyce, et al. Columbia, Album KC 33240. 1974.

One 33⅓ rpm record (2 sides). Side 1: Strike Up the Band (A Fieldsian Commercial), Fire in the Home, Life Among the Bolivians. Side 2: Tales of Michael Finn—A Tender Ballad, Romeo & Juliet, Scurvy Among the Extras, Jabberwocky & Etcetera.

843. ________. *From His Personal Collection. W. C. Fields Festival. The Great Radio Feuds.* W. C. Fields with Charlie McCarthy, Edgar Bergen and Don Ameche. Produced by Bruce Lundvall, Ted Joyce, et al. Columbia, Album KC 33241. 1974.

One 33⅓ rpm record (2 sides). Side 1: Communing with Nature, Father's Day. Side 2: The Golf Game, Elephants Et Al, Laughs Take a Holiday.

Note: In the Father's Day skit, Fields refers to being relieved of $12,000.00 (suit by Dr. Citron); some of his material is taken from his personal affairs at the time.

844. ________. *W. C. Fields. His Temperance Lecture and Promotions Unlimited 1930s. When Radio Was King!* Memorabilia Records, Album MLP-732. 1974.

One 33⅓ rpm record (2 sides).

845. ________. *Magnificent Rogue—The Adventures of W. C. Fields.* Narrated by Fred Allen. Exactly as heard on NBC radio's Biography in Sound, Feb. 28, 1956. Personality Series No. 1. Release No. 49. Radiola, Album MR-1049. 1975.

One 33⅓ rpm record (2 sides). Participants: William LeBaron, Robert Lewis Taylor, Leo McCarey, Uncle Jim Harkins, Maurice Chevalier, Mrs. George Kurimoto [Kitty Hughes], Errol Flynn, Ed Wynn, Ray Dooley, Mack Sennett, Ronald LeRoy Overacker (Baby LeRoy), Lester Cowan, Ann Ronnel [Mrs. Cowan], Norman Taurog, Edgar Bergen, and W. C. Fields excerpts from The Temperance Lecture (acknowledgement to Jay Records), plus Fields' The Day I Drank a Glass of Water, as heard on Request Performance with Ida Lupino and Reginald Gardner [sponsored by Campbell Soups, and produced by the Masquers Club of Hollywood].

846. ________. *W. C. Fields on Radio with Edgar Bergen & Charlie McCarthy.* The classic Fields-McCarthy battles plus complete performances from Fields' own [*sic*] radio shows. . . . Radio Yesteryear. Columbia, Album CS 9890. n.d. [circa 1975].

One 33⅓ rpm record (2 sides). Side 1: The Skunk Trap, Children, Old Friends and Old Wine, Feathered Friends, Moths, The Snake Story (a commercial). Side 2: Promotions Unlimited, The Swim to Catalina Island, The Pharmacist.

847. ________. *The Magic Radio.* A radio that tunes in programs of the past. One full hour of rare radio memories. Personality Series No. 2. Release No. 66. Radiola, Album MR-1066. 1976.

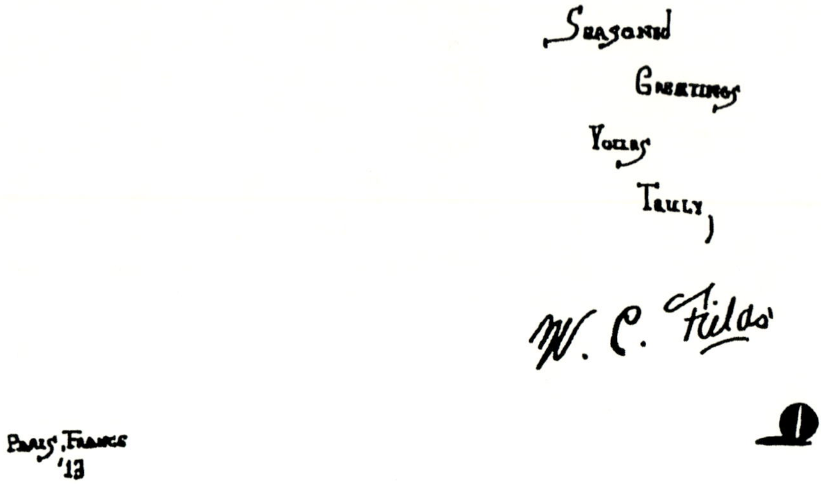

(inside of card) Xmas Card by W. C. Fields. Author's collection.

(front of card) Xmas Card by W. C. Fields. Author's collection.

One 33⅓ rpm record (2 sides). Side A: Moths. Side B: Fields not on this side.

848. ________. *W. C. Fields and Me.* Music and dialogue from the original motion picture soundtrack. Music composed and conducted by Henry Mancini. MCA Records, Album MCA-2092. 1976.

One 33⅓ rpm record (2 sides). Narrations by Valerie Perrine. Dialogue by Rod Steiger.

849. ________. *The Best of W. C. Fields.* Featuring excerpts from The Classic Fields-Charlie McCarthy Radio Feuds, The Further Adventures of Larson E. Whipsnade and Other Taradiddles, The Original Radio Adaptation of Fields' Monumental Film, "Poppy." A Petard Production. Columbia, Album CG 34144. 1976.

Two 33⅓ rpm records (4 sides). "This album consists of previously released material."

850. ________. *The Best of W. C. Fields.* Produced by Frank Bresee. Empala Records, Album EMP 101. 1978.

One 33⅓ rpm record (2 sides). Side 1: Swimming to Catalina, W. C. Fields Promotions Unlimited. Side 2: W. C. Fields' famous snake story, The Pharmacist.

851. ________. *The Murray Hill Radio Theatre. The Uncensored W. C. Fields. 1879[sic]–1946.* Celebrating the 100th birthday of a great American Comedian. W. C. Fields Productions, Inc. Murray Hill Records, Album M5467X. 1980.

Three 33⅓ rpm records (6 sides). Contains all previously recorded material. Side 4: "Fields with Eddie Cantor, Martha Raye, and Dick Powell." Eddie Cantor is not on this segment as advertised. The cut includes W. C. Fields, Dick Powell, Martha Raye, and Harry Einstein (Parkyakarkas). Einstein was previously a character actor on the Cantor show, but was not associated with Cantor at this time. This particular cut is a lead-in to Fields' A Tale of Michael Finn, A Tender Ballad.

852. ________. *W. C. Fields from Radio Program.* Collector item series. Wagner Research Corp., Microdisc 36M. n.d.

One 33⅓ rpm miniature record [same size as a 45 rpm] (1 side). A Tale of Michael Finn, A Tender Ballad.

853. ________. *W. C. Fields from Movie Sound Track.* Collector item series. Wagner Research Corp., Microdisc 39T. n.d.

One 33⅓ rpm miniature record (1 side). Sound tracks from David Copperfield, Poppy, Mississippi, Never Give a Sucker an Even Break, You Can't Cheat an Honest Man.

MISCELLANEOUS

Cigarette Cards

(All dates are Film Release Dates)

Over 2,000 series of cigarette cards were produced in the 1920s and 1930s, and only 11 to 17 sets were devoted to film stars. Fields' photo appeared on a total of 17 cards.

854. *Cinema Stars.* W. C. Fields. No. 18 of a series of 52 [black & white photo]. Printed in France. London: Godfrey Phillips Ltd., [1927].

"W. C. Fields was a clown at the Ziegfeld Follies in New York. D. W. Griffith the well known producer, noticed him and gave him a trial. Turned out to be the leading man in 'The skin of the lion.'" [American film title: *Running Wild*].

855. *Paramount Stars.* W. C. Fields. No. 14 of a series of 27 real photos [black & white photo]. London: Carreras High Class Cigarettes, [1928].

"W. C. Fields is one of the veterans of the American Stage. He has appeared in vaudeville and was at one time a comedy juggler. Among his early successes was 'Sally of the Sawdust' and more recent films include 'That Royale Girl,' 'The Old Army Game,' 'So's Your Old Man,' 'The Potters,' and 'Tillie's Punctured Romance.' Is 5 feet 8 inches tall and has red hair."

856. *Favourite Film Stars.* W. C. Fields. Paramount. No. 92 of a series of 96. London: Carreras Ltd., [1934].

"Real name William Claude Duganfield [*sic*]. Filled various jobs before making stage debut. Is born humourist who can introduce pathos without effort. Born in Philadelphia. Height 5 ft. 8 ins. Red hair, grey eyes. In 'It's a Gift' he appears with Baby LeRoy, and our picture is taken from that film."

857. *Famous Film Scenes.* W. C. Fields. 'David Copperfield.' A Metro-Goldwyn-Mayer Picture. No. 7 of a series of 48. London and Belfast: Gallaher Ltd., [1935].

"Here are W. C. Fields and Freddie Bartholomew as they appear in the film version of Charles Dicken's [*sic*] famous classic. There is an all-star cast in this film, but undoubtedly an outstanding performance is that of the former, as the improvident, but ever optimistic Micawber. Always besieged by creditors, he and his family are compelled at one time to enter a debtor's prison. Frank Lawton, who plays the part of David, when grown up, is also depicted with Maureen O'Sullivan in No. 34 of this series."

858. *Actors Natural & Character Studies.* "W. C. Fields as Wilkins Micawber in 'David Copperfield.'" No. 14 in a series of 50. Ogden's. Branch of the Imperial Tobacco Co. (of Great Britain & Ireland, Ltd), [1935].

"When Metro-Goldwyn-Mayer cast the Paramount star W. C. Fields for Mr. Micawber, the actor found himself so close in type to the part that he had hardly to make up at all. Clothes, in fact, made the man. This is odd, for Micawber ranks as a fantastic, while Mr. Fields (as this picture shows) has nothing eccentric in his appearance at all. But that is the way with Dickens. Apparently his people were caricatures; yet you meet their prototypes everywhere you go."

859. *Film Favourites.* W. C. Fields (Paramount). No. 71 in a series of 100 pictures. London: A. and M. Wix, [1935].

"W. C. Fields is a comedian of ripe vintage—in his music hall days he was probably the cleverest juggler of his time—he is always smiling. Curiously enough he did not reach success in the old silent days, although he is essentially a pantomimist, and there was a time when neither work nor money came his way. Unlike most funny men, he has no desire to play Hamlet, and nowadays all his eggs are not in one basket, because he raises chickens and makes a 'bit on the side' with fruits and vegetables. His best known success is Micawber in the film 'David Copperfield.'"

860. *Cinema Cavalcade.* W. C. Fields and Freddie Bartholomew. David Copperfield. (Courtesy of Metro-Goldwyn-Mayer).

State whether English or Afrikaans edition is preferred. No. 184 of a series of 250 pictures with 50 in full color [black & white photo]. Johannesburg: Max Cigarettes, [1935].

South African card, 6.8cm × 13cm, over-size, in two languages. British cigarette cards are normally 3.5cm × 6.5cm.

"W. C. Fields as Micawber, a part well suited to his loquacious talents. Freddie Bartholomew, as the Author's favourite child, David Copperfield."

861. *Post Card.* W. C. Fields and Freddie Bartholomew. This is No. 10 of a series of cards appearing in the larger packings of De Reszke Cigarettes and other Godfrey Phillips Associated brands. [Johannesburg]: De Reszke Cigarettes, [1935].

Card is in full color, over-size 8.9cm × 12.6cm. Total cards in series is not given.

"Two of the best remembered performances of the year were given by W. C. Fields, the Paramount contract star, and Freddie Bartholomew in 'David Copperfield' (M-G-M). Fields has had a distinguished career as a comedian in vaudeville, musical comedy and films. Freddie Bartholomew, a ten year old London boy, was selected out of 10,000 applicants for the title role of 'David Copperfield,' in which he created a sensation. Is under contract to M-G-M, playing with Garbo in 'Anna Karenina' and also the title role of Kipling's 'Kim.'"

862. *Cinema Cavalcade.* 'You've said a mouthful.' Mississippi. (Courtesy of Paramount Pictures). No. 157 in a series of 250 pictures. . . . Johannesburg: Max Cigarettes, [1935].

Over-size card, 5.5cm × 7.5cm. Black & white photo.

"W. C. Fields, as captain of a show-boat on the Mississippi, arrogantly scorns the threats of one of his creditors (Fred Kohler) while attending to the requirements of the inner man, aided by his mint julep at his side."

863. *Film Episodes.* W. C. Fields. No. 4 in a series of 48. 'The Memory Expert.' (Paramount). London & Belfast: Gallaher Ltd., [1935].

"W. C. Fields and Mary Brian in a scene from 'The Memory Expert,' a typical Fields' comedy, in which he appears as a bewildered and henpecked husband who gets himself involved in the most extraordinary situations. His adventures with burglars who invade his house, and how he goes to a wrestling match on the pretext of his mother-in-law's funeral, provide a wealth of comedy. Mary Brian gives a very attractive performance as his daughter." [American film title: Man on the Flying Trapeze.]

864. *Famous Film Stars.* W. C. Fields (A Paramount Star). No. 22 in a series of 50. Issued with Milky Way Bars by Mars Confections Ld. Slough. [Buckinghamshire]: Mars Confections, [1936].

"In a cramped boarding house room in Atlantic City many years ago, a youngster known as Claude William Dukenfield finished the task of combing his hair and began the simpler task of counting his earnings for the day. His day's receipts, in pennies and nickels, came to less than one dollar. Papers were hard to sell in off season. The count completed, the future William C. Fields tossed his comb into the air, followed it with a nickel and a penny and went into his evening's practice at juggling. It was thus that he embarked upon his career which has led him to the top of the stage and to his unparalleled position on the screen."

865. *Cinema Cavalcade.* My Little Plumb! W. C. Fields and Rochelle Hudson in 'Poppy.' (Courtesy of Paramount Pictures). No. 155 of a series of 250. Johannesburg: Max Cigarettes, [1936].

Black & white photo. Regular size card.

866. *Cinema Cavalcade.* 'Hot Dogs.' Poppy. No. 156 of a series of 250. Johannesburg: Max Cigarettes, [1936].

Black & white photo. Regular size card.

"With a lordly gesture, W. C. Fields orders a meal for himself and daughter, while poor Poppy (Rochelle Hudson) wonders how they will pay for it." (Courtesy Paramount Pictures).

867. *From Screen and Stage.* Rochelle Hudson and W. C. Fields in Poppy (Paramount). No. 17. [London]: Ardath Tobacco Co., Ltd., [1936].

Over-size card, 6.8cm × 9.5cm, in full color. Total cards in series not given.

"Droll W. C. Fields is one of the most popular of screen comedians. Born in Philadelphia he started work at an early age and filled various positions before entering vaudeville when still in his 'teens. Years later he appeared in Ziegfeld's Follies and then made several silent films. Sandy-haired and a great humourist, Fields rose from a sick bed to star with Rochelle Hudson in 'Poppy.' Petite Rochelle Hudson, a native of Oklahoma, is a hard-working young actress who climbed the ladder to fame entirely on her merits. She had had no previous experience of acting when at the age of 16 she was offered small parts in Hollywood. She played her first important role in 'Top of the Bill' and has since starred in several successful productions."

868. *Film Favourites.* Constance Moore and W. C. Fields in 'You Can't Cheat an Honest Man.' (Courtesy of Universal Pictures). No. 94. Third series of 100 pictures. London: A. and M. Wix, [1939].

"Constance Moore sang with an orchestra and appeared in radio programmes before taking up screen work. She has a good many pictures to her credit, including 'The Crime of Dr. Hallet,' 'Swing that Cheer,' 'Prison Break,' and 'The Missing Guest.'

"W. C. Fields scarcely needs introduction; his real name is William Claude Dukenfield, and he has been famous since Ziegfeld Follies days. Latest films include 'Poppy,' 'The Big Broadcast,' 'David Copperfield,' and 'Mississippi.' He is also an author of note."

869. *Cinema Cavalcade.* A Double Crossing Dummy. You Can't Cheat an Honest Man. (Courtesy Universal Pictures). No. 159 in a series of 250 pictures. Johannesburg: Max Cigarettes, [1939].

Black & white photo. 5.5cm × 7.6cm.

"Circus proprietor Larson E. Whipsnade (W. C. Fields) eyes Edgar Bergen's dummy (Charlie McCarthy) with distaste, Charlie has stolen from the till [*sic*] with Whipsnade has stolen from his gullible patrons. Edgar has a black eye—Whipsnade had a hand in that, too."

870. *Cinema Cavalcade.* The Whip Hand. W. C. Fields and Constance Moore. You Can't Cheat an Honest Man. (Courtesy Universal Pictures.) No. 158 of a series of 250. Johannesburg: Max Cigarettes, [1939].

Black & white photo. 5.5cm × 7.6cm.

Film Clips

AS MOVIES

871. 1949. Eagle-Lion. *Down Memory Lane.*

872. 1951. Columbia. *Memories of Famous Hollywood Comedians.*

873. 1964. M-G-M. *Big Parade of Comedy.*

874. 1976. M-G-M/United Artists. *That's Entertainment, Part II.*

AS VIDEO TAPES

875. SRO 9010. *Look Who's Laughing.* Trailers from WCF films *My Little Chickadee, The Bank Dick, You Can't Cheat an Honest Man,* and M-G-M's *Big Parade of Comedy.*

876. SRO 9024. *Classic Movie Bloopers.* Fields on the set of *International House* during the 1933 earthquake and a clip from *The Dentist.*

877. VCI 7001. *Brother, Can You Spare a Dime?* Fields on the set of *The Big Broadcast of 1938;* one clip with Mitch Leisen, and two clips of WCF alone.

878. Budget Video. *Hollywood, My Home Town.* Original film by Ken Murray. Fields outside his dressing room at Universal Studios.

AS TELEVISION SPECIALS

879. March 23, 1967. CBS. Camera Three. *W. C. Fields Rediscovered,* featuring W. C. Fields, Jr. 60 minutes.

880. Unknown 1969. Made for television. *Silent Night, Lonely Night.* Drama with Lloyd Bridges, Shirley Jones, Lynn Carlin, Cloris Leachman. Background in film, clip from *The Bank Dick.* 2 hours.

881. Unknown. 1978. Made for television. *Funny Business.* Hosted by Walter Matthau. Fields clip from *My Little Chickadee.* 2 hours, 5 minutes.

882. May 16, 1982. ABC. Made for television. *Hollywood: The Gift of Laughter.* Narrated by Carol Burnett, Dom DeLuise, Jack Lemon, Walter Matthau, Richard Prior, and Burt Reynolds. Clips from *The Dentist, The Bank Dick, Six of a Kind, The Old Fashioned Way, Tillie & Gus, It's a Gift, The Barber Shop, My Little Chickadee,* and *Million Dollar Legs.* 3 hours.

883. May 19, 1982. Made for public television. *Great Radio Comedians.* Film clips, stills, and broadcast tapes of Bergen and McCarthy, W. C. Fields, Mae West, and Clark Gable. 90 minutes.

884. April 4, 1984. NBC. Bob Hope's *Who Makes the World Laugh—Part II.* Clip from *My Little Chickadee.* 60 minutes.

885. March 8, 1986. Public television. *W. C. Fields Straight Up.* Narrated by Dudley Moore. A profile of Fields with clips from *It's a Gift, Poppy, The Bank Dick, Never Give a Sucker an Even Break.* 90 minutes.

886. No date. Public television. *Those Fabulous Clowns.* Narrated by Richard Kiley. Clips from *Pool Sharks, Sally of the Sawdust, The Golf Specialist, The Dentist,* and *Poppy.* 90 minutes.

Impersonators

The earliest impersonations of Fields were in film cartoons, beginning of 1934, followed by John Sinclair, Fields' movie double in Poppy, *1936. The first actor to impersonate Fields on radio was Bill Thompson, who played "Horatio K. Boomer" on the* Fibber McGee & Molly *program, 1937–38.*

Since his death, at least seven persons have professionally impersonated Fields' voice, and or mannerisms:

887. Rod Steiger.

Rod Steiger as a psychopath in the film *No Way to Treat*

a Lady, 1968, and, as W. C. Fields in the film *W. C. Fields and Me*, 1976.

888. Bill Oberlin.

Prelutsky, Burt. "Deja Nose. W. C. Fields Is Alive and Well in Bill Oberlin." L.A. Times *West Magazine* (7 Feb. 1971): 5.

889. Rich Little.

Rich Little as W. C. Fields for President; a comedy album. Caedmon Records, 1972.

890. Ted Allison.

Carter, Tom. "Playing Bill Has Become Full Career." Santa Ana Register *Leisuretime* (27 Jan. 1974): 18–19.

891. Bramwell Young.

Anderson, Jess, Jr. "Commemorating the Comic." (Photo.) *Daily News Tribune* (30 Jan. 79): A-7.

892. Chuck McCann.

Chuck McCann in the television movie "Mae West," 30-18 *T. V. Guide* (1–7 May 1982): A-41.

McCann also appears in commercials as W. C. Fields.

893. Tom Blankenship.

Blankenship claims that he "can now legally be called W. C. Fields." *Star* (16 Jan. 1990): 5.

INDEX